How to Apply the Right Choice Model

Create a Right-Minded Team That Works as One

Do No Harm.
Work As One.

By
Dan Hogan
Certified Master Facilitator

Books by Dan Hogan

Reason, Ego, & the Right-Minded Teamwork Myth: *The Philosophy and Process for Creating a Right-Minded Team That Works Together as One*

Right-Minded Teamwork in Any Team: *The Ultimate Team Building Method to Create a Team That Works as One*

How to Facilitate Team Work Agreements: *A Practical, 10-Step Process for Building a Right-Minded Team That Works as One*

How to Apply the Right Choice Model:
Create a Right-Minded Team That Works as One

7 Mindfulness Training Lessons: *Improve Teammates' Ability to Work as One with Right-Minded Thinking*

Right-Minded Teamwork:
9 Right Choices for Building a Team That Works as One

Design a Right-Minded, Team-Building Workshop:
12 Steps to Create a Team That Works as One

Achieve Your Organization's Strategic Plan: *Create a Right-Minded Team Management System to Ensure All Teams Work as One*

Copyright © 2021, 2025 by Dan Hogan, Lord & Hogan LLC. All rights reserved.

Contact Dan Hogan at Dan.Hogan@RightMindedTeamwork.com

This book is licensed for personal, non-commercial use only. No part of this publication may be reproduced, distributed, or transmitted in any form or by any means, including photocopying, recording, or other electronic or mechanical methods, without the prior written permission of the publisher, except for brief quotations embodied in critical reviews and certain other noncommercial uses permitted by copyright law.

ISBN: 978-1-939585-10-3

Acknowledgments & Appreciations

To the thousands of teammates, team leaders, and team-building facilitators with whom I've worked with over the last 40 years,

Thank You

For being my teacher.

Collectively, we created this awesome team-building program.

Right-Minded Teamwork is a business-oriented, psychological approach to team building where acceptance, forgiveness, and adjustment are teammate characteristics, and customer satisfaction is the team's result.

In addition, there are several special people I want to joyfully acknowledge and thank for their contributions.

First and foremost, I want to convey my deep and heartfelt gratitude to our editor, Erin Leigh. Thanks to her superb editing and vital guidance, Right-Minded Teamwork is now much easier to understand and successfully integrate into your team. Thank you, Erin. The RMT book series would not have happened without you.
(To contact Erin, email erin@thechoice.life.)

Next, a giant thank you to the Ebook Launch team. Dane Low, our book cover designer, created exceptional cover designs for the Right-Minded Teamwork book series. Thank you for elevating Right-Minded Teamwork. (To reach Dane visit EbookLaunch.com.)

Another sincere thank you goes out to Cathi Bosco, our graphic artist, who renovated and modernized many of our Right-Minded Teamwork process models, graphics, and illustrations
(reach her at CathiBosco.com).
And I also want to thank the Media A-Team, who created the original and current versions of the Right Choice Model
(find them at Mediaateam.com).

Finally, I want to express my gratitude to Jackie D'Elia, our website and UX designer, who successfully modernized the RightMindedTeamwork.com website into an easy-to-use platform. Her work allows us to share the RMT books, models, and other resources and materials with the world. Thank you, Jackie.
(Contact Jackie at JackieDElia.com.)

CONTENTS

Preface 15
What Is Right Choice? 27
    Choosing Your Team's Right Attitudes & Behaviors 29

How Does a Team Use the Right Choice Model? 61
Right Choice & Your Team Work Agreements 71
Right Choice as a Personal Tool 77
Right Choice: Step-by-Step Application 79
How to Present & Apply the Right Choice Model in Your Team 99
Applications for the Right Choice Model 107
Everything Else About the Right Choice Model 111

The End. Your New Beginning. 143
About the Author 147
    Books by Dan Hogan 150

Glossary of Right-Minded Teamwork Terms & Resources 154
  100% Customer Satisfaction 154
  7 Mindfulness Training Lessons 154
  10 Characteristics of Right-Minded Teammates........................... 155
  12 Steps Workshop Design Process 156
  A Course in Miracles 156
  Accept, Forgive, Adjust 157
  Ally or Adversary Teammate.. 158
  Avoidance Behavior.. 159
  Battleground: Where People Are Punished for Mistakes............. 160
  Certified Master Facilitator (CMF).. 161
  Classroom: Where People Learn from Mistakes 161
  Communication Work Agreement 162
  Create, Promote, Allow... 163
  Critical Few: Complete Important Tasks First.............................. 163
  Decision-Maker: The Real You 164
  Decision-Maker: Trust Your Intuition 165
  Decision-Making Work Agreement 166
  Desire & Willingness: Preconditions for Accountability.............. 167
  Do No Harm. Work as One... 168
  Ego & Ego Attack 169
  Interlocking Accountability 170
  Moment of Reason 171
  Onboarding New Teammates.. 171
  Oneness vs. Separateness.. 172
  Preventions & Interventions... 173
  Psychological Goals 174
  Reason... 175
  Reason, Ego & the Right-Minded Teamwork Myth 176
  Recognition: Make It Easy to Keep Going 177

Right Choice Model 178
Right-Minded Teamwork's 5-Element Framework 179
Right-Minded Teamwork's 5 Element Implementation Plan....... 180
Right-Minded Teamwork Attitudes & Behaviors 181
Right-Mindedness vs. Wrong-Mindedness 182
RMT Facilitator 183
Team Management System: An RMT Enterprise-Wide Process . 184
Team Operating System & Performance Factor Assessment....... 185
Thought System 186
Train Your Mind... 187
Uncovering Root Cause.. 188
Unified Circle of Right-Minded Thinking................................... 189
Work Agreements... 190

Resources... 191

RightMinded TEAMWORK Choice Model

Right-Minded Accountability
- Forgive
- Accept
- Acknowledge
- Recover
- Adjust

Difficult Situation → Internal Decision-Maker → CHOICE

Victim/Victimizer
- Retreat
- Defend
- Attack
- Reject
- Avoid

Praise for the Right Choice Model

I actually have [the Right Choice Model] card pinned with magnets to my file cabinet, and I refer to it routinely to coach myself and others in difficult situations. It has helped us to create a positive attitude in our teamwork. **Dave Jenson**

I have a Right Choice Model poster in my office and a card in my wallet that I use frequently when managing conflict and providing coaching to others. It is a valuable tool that has made my job and personal life easier. **Danny Boyd**

I'm looking at a Right Choice Model poster in my office as I type this note and appreciate you bringing this into my career and personal life. I don't think a day goes by that I don't think about this Model or share the principles with someone. **Jacob Gros**

I have been using your Right Choice Model in most of my workshops since 2005. I enjoy it, am inspired by it, and find it very useful. For team-building activities, Right Choice is most definitely highly recommended. **Teca Pedro**

I've used the Right Choice Model for 20+ years and still live by the process today in my professional and personal life. It's a great way to kick-start a new team or invigorate a seasoned one. **Ken McCall**

I can tell you without a doubt that my team and I use the Right Choice Model all we can and we LOVE it!! Our team has really grown and achieved a lot through the program, and we continue each week in our meetings to utilize what you have taught us. **Cindy Thomas**

Preface

Welcome to Right-Minded Teamwork (RMT).

What is RMT?

Right-Minded Teamwork is an intelligent and empowering teamwork system that creates a *team that works together as one*.

Every one of us has the right to experience the magic that can happen when teammates work together as *one unified team*. Each of us can claim and exercise that right, starting right now, if we choose. That is why RMT is for everyone, everywhere, forever. And, through these pages, it is available to you.

Apply RMT, and you will improve your work processes and strengthen your relationships.

Apply RMT, and your team will achieve 100% customer satisfaction.

Apply RMT, and your team will *work together as one*.

You'll also do your part to make the world a better place for everyone, everywhere, forever.

Let's get started right now.

It is an honor to introduce you to Right-Minded Teamwork's **Right Choice Model** and teaching process. This real-world, team-building, teaching aid has improved the lives and teams of thousands of people worldwide.

Apply the Right Choice in your team, and you, too, will reap its benefits.

Before we get started, let me answer a few questions that may be on your mind.

What Is "Right" in Right-Minded Teamwork?

RMT has nothing to do with right-brain thinking or right-wing viewpoints.

It has everything to do with what your team, together, decides is "right." Your team's choices, identified collectively, define your team's Right-Minded attitudes and work behaviors.

*The "right" way is the way you **choose** is right for your team.*

So, how do you open up a team discussion about what is right or wrong for your team?

You start by introducing the Right Choice Model.

What is the Right Choice Model?

The Right Choice Model is a tool to help you and your teammates make the conscious choice to follow your team's Right-Minded attitudes and behaviors.

HOW TO APPLY THE RIGHT CHOICE MODEL · 17

The Right Choice Model consists of two parts. The first part is a graphic illustration of the Choice Model that depicts its "upper loop" and "lower loop." The second part of the Model is an important, Right-Minded question you will use when difficult situations arise.

For easy reference, you will find both the graphic illustration of the Right Choice Model and the important, Right-Minded question on the Right Choice cards. These three-by-four-inch templates are designed for easy printing and distribution to teammates.

To download RMT models and materials to give teammates, go to RightMindedTeamwork.com, and search for this book's companion **Reusable Resources & Templates**.

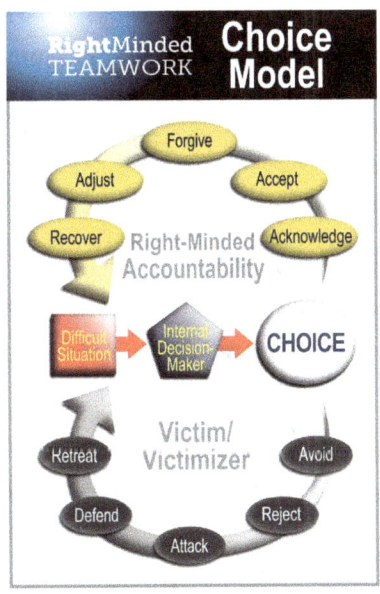
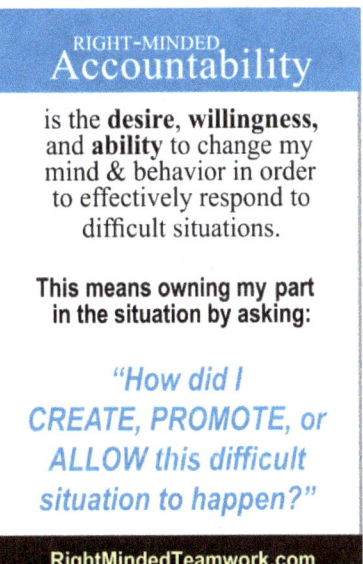

As you can see in the images above, the upper loop of the Model describes Right-Minded accountability, and the lower loop defines wrong-minded victimization. The definition of Right-Minded accountability and the important, Right-Minded question, found on the back of the Right Choice cards, are the tools you use to move you and your teammates back into your Right Minds.

Right Choice promotes the concept that every person has free will. Free will means you are 100% responsible for how you respond to every situation, circumstance, and event that happens.

When difficult team situations occur, you either:
1. act as an ally, choosing to demonstrate accountable, responsible, and Right-Minded behaviors
2. choose to be adversarial, react to difficult situations by becoming a victim or victimizer, and demonstrate wrong-minded behaviors

Wrong choices lead to victimization, blame, and punishment among teammates. They guarantee solutions are not found because teammates are too busy pointing fingers at others and defending themselves.

Right-Minded Choices are the only sane response to challenging team situations. Why? Because teammates who demonstrate the Right actions and behaviors find real solutions to their problems.

In another RMT book, *Reason, Ego, and the Right-Minded Teamwork Myth,* you are introduced to three characters: Reason, Ego, and you, the Decision-Maker. Their story, the Right-Minded Teamwork Myth, illustrates the origin of the Right-Minded Teamwork philosophy and Right Choice.

Simply put, the RMT Myth advocates for teammates to follow Reason's path to oneness and shared interest instead of following Ego's disastrous advice to seek separateness and prioritize selfishness.

Following Reason is the Right Choice every time.

Later in this book, you will find a list of 30 of Reason's Right-Minded Teamwork attitudes and behaviors that your team can adapt and adopt to create your own team thought system. In that section, you will also see Ego's list of wrong-minded choices.

EGO

DECISION MAKER

REASON

In the RMT book ***Right-Minded Teamwork in Any Team***: *The Ultimate Team Building Method to Create a Team That Works as One*, I share the following RMT definition:

> *Right-Minded Teamwork is a business-oriented, psychological approach to team building where acceptance, forgiveness, and adjustment are teammate characteristics, and 100% customer satisfaction is the team's result.*

When you adapt Right Choice attitudes and behaviors in your team, you automatically demonstrate acceptance, forgiveness, and adjustment. Your team readily embodies the exact characteristics that help you achieve 100% customer satisfaction.

Welcome to Your New Role: RMT Leader and Facilitator

I want to take a moment to congratulate you on your new role. Incorporating the Right Choice Model into your team-building repertoire means **you are now a Right-Minded Teamwork Leader and Facilitator.**

As an RMT Facilitator, **your specialty is team transformations**.

Using RMT's Right Choice Model, you help to transform dysfunctional souls into healthy and functional teammates. You guide teammates to convert their mistakes into Right-Minded attitudes and behaviors. They express their deep and heartfelt gratitude for your facilitation efforts and results. Some even say you "saved them," continuing to seek your support for years to come.

Whether you're new to facilitation or continuing to build your team-building toolkit, add RMT to your practice today. There's no reason not to: All parts of Right-Minded Teamwork, including the Right Choice Model and Work Agreements, are available for your use. There are no licensing or certification requirements.

My only request is that you accept Reason's wisdom on this path. With Reason's guidance, you can easily apply these methods to help your teams create and sustain Right-Minded Teamwork.

My Special Support Function

It took countless workshops, a 35-year career in active team-building facilitation, and the collective wisdom of so many teammates and team leaders to conceptualize and build Right-Minded Teamwork into the robust model it is today.

Though I no longer facilitate actively, choosing to pass that torch on to the next generation of facilitators, I will always continue to promote Right-Minded Teamwork.

The reason for my continued passion is quite simple. I know, beyond a shadow of a doubt, that RMT and the Right Choice Model are right for every team, everywhere, forever. If you use them, they will help make your client team(s) and the world a better place. To make that happen, though, **your clients need you to show them and their teams the Right-Minded Teamwork way.**

As you lead them down the RMT path, remember: I am here to support you. So, reach out to me. Ask me questions. Let me get to know you so I can refer you to clients looking for an RMT Facilitator.

Also remember that even though you will undoubtedly help your client teams achieve an "early win," creating and sustaining Right-Minded Teamwork takes at least a year.

So, as you enter into the team-building process, stick with it for the long haul. Plan to stay with your team(s) for at least one to two years. Help them firmly establish RMT in their team. Give them the foundation they need to learn, grow, and succeed.

As you do, you *will do your part to make the world a better place for everyone, everywhere, forever.*

Overview:
How to Present & Apply the Right Choice Model in Your Team

When you first present the Right Choice concepts in a team-building workshop, your objective is to help your team embrace Right-Minded accountability as a way to overcome their team challenges. Your goal is to present the Right Choice Model in such a way that when you finish teaching it, all teammates declare,

> *"Of course, we need to approach [our difficult situation] in a Right-Minded, accountable way. Let's get started."*

It's best to stick with a short presentation. Four to five minutes will suffice.

As soon as all teammates are in the right frame of mind, stop presenting, and move everyone into a team discussion about the problematic team issue.

In that conversation, encourage teammates to use their Right attitudes of accepting, forgiving, and adjusting behaviors while discussing the issue. Some teammates will not be as skilled as others. That's okay; they don't need to be. Thoroughly learning the Model's concepts in the first presentation is not your aim.

This team discussion eventually leads to creating team Work Agreements. We'll talk more about Work Agreements later, but for now, think of them as team statements that all teammates believe will resolve the issue at hand. After the workshop, teammates follow their Work Agreements, working together in their new, agreed-upon way. Increased productivity follows, and, in time, your team has even happier customers.

In summary, applying the Right Choice process includes these steps:

1. Present the Right Choice Model to your teammates and gain their commitment to accept, forgive, and adjust their attitudes and behaviors
2. Conduct a team talk to find solutions
3. Capture your solutions in team Work Agreements
4. Follow your Work Agreements to improve teamwork and increase productivity
5. Enjoy happier customers!

**Overview:
What's in This Book**

The remainder of this book will expand on and explore the Right Choice Model steps summarized above.

First, we will discuss some of the pivotal concepts of the Right Choice Model including choice, intuition, mindfulness, and the Unified Circle of Right-Minded Thinking.

Next, we will learn the three options for applying the Right Choice Model in your team. For all three options, you will want to print the **Right Choice cards** and give them to your teammates.

Reminder:
To download RMT models and materials to give teammates, go to RightMindedTeamwork.com, and search for this book's companion **Reusable Resources & Templates**.

After that, you'll find a broader explanation of the Right Choice concepts, including two effective, thorough application methods: 1) how to apply the Right Choice Model in your life, and 2) how to present and apply it in your team.

You'll also discover a list of 30 Right-Minded Teamwork attitudes and behaviors. This is a useful resource list of behavioral concepts that your team can adapt and then adopt.

From there, we will review a robust list of other applications for Right Choice. Once you start using this Model, you will discover many opportunities to apply it.

Finally, for those of you who love comprehensive explanations, you will find two more sections of interest: *Everything Else About the Right Choice Model* and a complete *Glossary of Right-Minded Teamwork Terms & Resources*.

Before we go any farther, I'd like to make you a sincere and Right-Minded offer.

If you need clarification or just desire a little more coaching on applying the Right Choice Model in your team or organization, I invite you to contact me. Even though I'm retired from active team facilitation, I am here to support you, and I'm available to help you succeed. If you have questions, please don't hesitate to send me a message. Really! Dan.Hogan@RightMindedTeamwork.com.

Let's get started. ~ Dan Hogan

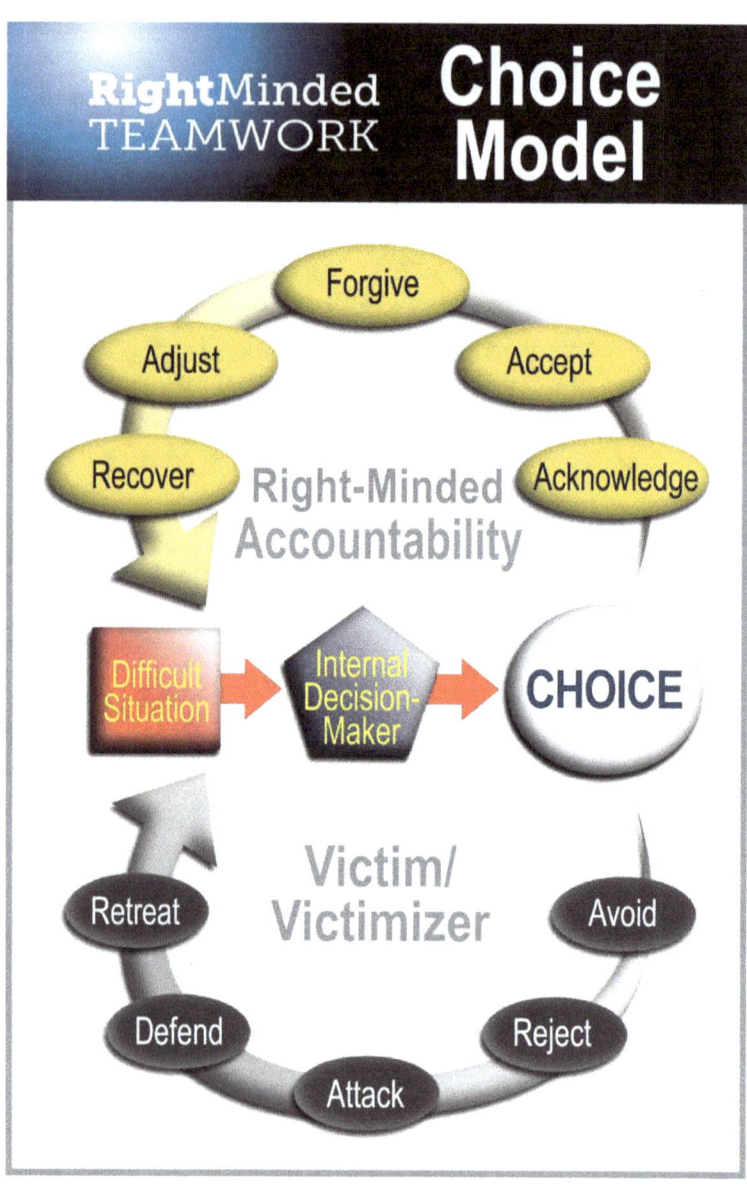

What Is Right Choice?

Teammates who band together and choose accountability over victimization create Right-Minded Teamwork.

The key word here is "choose." If you want to do your part to strengthen teammate bonds, you must choose to train your mind to consistently apply the lessons taught in the Right Choice Model.

You must choose to follow and live the attitudes and behaviors, as described in your Work Agreements, that define how all teammates will **do no harm** and **work as one**.

What Is Choice?

Choice is your inner power. It is your right and liberty to react as you please to life's difficult situations.

Depending on how you respond, you either make difficult situations better or worse. You know this is true; you have your own experiences as proof.

You respond to all situations with:
- your attitude – your inward choice
- your behavior – your outward choice

Choice, as presented in this Model, is a "thinking system" for people who want to use their minds to effectively address the root cause of poor and non-productive behavior in themselves and others.

Choice always precedes behavior.

Attitude always precedes choice.

Choosing Your Team's
Right Attitudes & Behaviors

To achieve Right-Minded Teamwork, your team must first identify its "right" attitudes. Those attitudes form your team's collective, consciously chosen **thought system**. They describe how you will **do no harm** as you **work as one**.

Your team's initial set of Right-Minded attitudes is agreed upon during your first workshop. After that, they may be adjusted and updated on an as-needed basis.

How to Choose Right-Minded Attitudes for Your Team

Your list of "right" attitudes can be short. Here is an example.

We choose these Right-Minded attitudes as our psychological goals:
- *We accept 100% accountability and responsibility for our thoughts and behaviors.*
- *When we make mistakes, we never punish. We learn. We recover. We do no harm. We work as one.*
- *We positively acknowledge and reward each other.*
- *We are we-centered, never self-centered.*
- *When difficult team situations happen, we accept, forgive, and adjust our attitudes and behavior. We always find solutions because we believe that none of us is as smart as all of us.*
- *When new teammates join our team, we will share these goals and ask them to choose them, too.*

After you create these values and norms, you will commit to actively living them. Your attitudes and commitment to living them are transformed into your team's written Work Agreements.

Two Options for Choosing Attitudes & Behaviors

You have two options for identifying the "right" attitudes and psychological goals for your team. Feel free to use both.

1. Share the **Right-Minded Teammate Attitudes & Behaviors** list with the team (see below), and allow teammates to choose a few from that list, or use those ideas to create goals that fit your team better.

2. Share the **Right Choice Model** in this book. In a team event, agree on a list of accountable attitudes and work behaviors your team believes are needed to address your teamwork issues and sustain Right-Minded Teamwork.

You Have Only Two Response Choices

The Right-Minded Choice Model teaches that you are the **Decision-Maker**, and you only have two choices regarding how you respond to every difficult situation.

When a challenging situation happens, you either:
- accept Ego's guidance and act like a victim or victimizer, or
- embrace Reason and act in an accountable, Right-Minded way, as described in your team Work Agreements.

Even though there are many variations of those two choices, *there are still just two.*

At all times, you are mindful, or you are mindless. You are either following your Right Mind, Reason, or your wrong mind, Ego.

For the background story behind the **RMT Choice Model**, read RMT's ***Reason, Ego, and the Right-Minded Teamwork Myth***. This story introduces the three characters who live in every teammate's life: Reason, Ego, and the Decision-Maker.

You Are the Decision-Maker

The Right-Minded Choice Model says "you" are your own internal Decision-Maker.

This "you" is your observer, interpreter, and decider. It is the part of you that sees all your experiences and determines how you will respond to those situations.

Look closely at the Right Choice Model now.

Do you see yourself, the Decision-Maker, sitting right in the middle between your difficult situation and the choice you must make?

In this position, between the difficult situation you are facing and the choice you must make, you are faced with two choices. You either choose the Right direction – as described in your Work Agreements – or the wrong direction.

As the Decision-Maker, you are never alone during these moments of choice. Reason and Ego are always there in your mind, whether you are conscious of them or not. Each time you make a decision, you either mindfully and consciously choose to follow your team's Work Agreements, or you mindlessly and unconsciously decide to follow Ego's lessons and wrong-minded thinking.

Choosing the upper loop of the Right Choice Model means **accepting**, **forgiving**, and **adjusting** your thoughts and behaviors. In doing so, you move into the Unified Circle of Right-Minded Thinking. In contrast, choosing the lower loop of rejection, Ego attack, and defensiveness takes you into the divided circle of wrong-minded thinking.

Right-Minded Teamwork upholds the upper circle of the Right Choice Model.

For more about Right-Minded attitudes, see the Right-Minded Teamwork Attitudes & Behaviors list in the pages that follow.

Trust Your Intuition as the Decision-Maker

If thinking about Reason and Ego is new to you, it can be helpful to think of Reason as your positive intuition and Ego as your negative, arrogant, and sometimes vindictive intuition.

At different times throughout our lives, we all listen to and follow each of these teachers.

Stop and remember when you had a hunch or feeling about what you should do or say in a particular situation. Did you ignore your intuition? Let's say you did not follow your instinct, and it turned out to be a mistake. What did you say to yourself and others?

> *I wish I had trusted my intuition!*

As this memory illustrates, **you already know how to listen and be mindful** of your intuition. Following Reason is your natural, pre-separation state of mind. You just need to do it regularly.

If not…

Remember a time when you became angry, agitated, or annoyed with a teammate. Without thinking, you said mean-spirited things. You were saying to yourself, "My life can't get better until you change." Your negative behavior happened because you did not stop for a **moment of Reason**.

You were literally **out of your Right Mind** as you unconsciously turned towards Ego for guidance.

EGO **DECISION MAKER** **REASON**

During your reaction, you were mindless as you followed Ego's advice. Then, after a while, once you stepped back and calmed down, you could see your behavior was a mistake - only a mistake, to be corrected, not punished. At this moment, you shifted your perspective. You forgave yourself, and you adjusted by apologizing and promising not to behave that way again. You returned to your Right Mind.

If you are not accustomed to trusting your intuition but would like to do so more, you will need to practice.

> *The key is to **pause**, be **still**, and intentionally **listen** for your positive intuition - that **moment of Reason** - before you react to a situation or event.*

It is that simple. But that does not make it easy, especially at first. It takes mindful practice to train your mind to listen for this joyous, intuitive moment. It takes an unwavering commitment to stop yourself continually, gently, and compassionately when you become angry, fearful, agitated, or anxious.

It is not always easy, but it can be done. Many have learned this skill. You can, too. As the Decision-Maker, you always have free will regarding whether you choose to follow Ego or Reason. Even if you've tried before and failed, you can start again today.

Remember that even with steadfast commitment, it will take practice to excel. You will make mistakes. That's okay. Choose Reason again. Choose to follow your Work Agreements again. And again, and again. When you realize you've chosen Ego, apologize, forgive, correct, forget the mistake, and move on. The more you practice, the easier it will get.

You will soon find that as you change your mind, you automatically change your behavior. And when you change your behavior, you transform your team into a lovely learning classroom. The more you make an effort to *be* **in your Right Mind,** the easier it will become to *stay* **in your Right Mind**.

Now, instead of saying, *"I wish I had listened to my intuition,"* you will say,

I'm so glad I turned towards Reason and followed my intuition!

EGO

DECISION MAKER

REASON

Mindfulness Is Choice in Action

When you are mindless, you don't think or reflect. Instead of consciously choosing how to respond, you react unconsciously in an emotionally immature way, blaming others or avoiding the situation altogether.

When you're mindful, you reflect and carefully choose how you respond to everything that happens to you and around you. When a problematic situation happens, being mindful means asking yourself this question that is in the model:

*What did I do or say to **create**, **promote**, or **allow** this to happen?*

Your answers to this question help you and your team experience a **moment of Reason,** which paves the way for you to create real solutions.

As an example, let's assume a significant mistake has happened in your team.

Half the team is aggressively blaming the other half for the mistake in what is often called an **"Ego attack."**

> RIGHT-MINDED
> **Accountability**
> is the **desire, willingness,** and **ability** to change my mind & behavior in order to effectively respond to difficult situations.
>
> **This means owning my part in the situation by asking:**
>
> *"How did I CREATE, PROMOTE, or ALLOW this difficult situation to happen?"*
>
> RightMindedTeamwork.com

Teammates are making toxic and hurtful statements, directly and indirectly, about each other. The team is stuck in a battleground of "attack and defend." No one is working to resolve the mistake.

Seeking a **moment of Reason**, you ask yourself,

> *What am I doing to create, promote, or allow this blaming conversation to continue?*

You realize you've been standing by and saying nothing. You were **avoiding**, which is the **first step in the lower loop** of the Right Choice Model.

Now that you are aware of your attitude and behavior, you change your mind. You choose to follow Reason and act in a Right-Minded, accountable way, just as your Work Agreement states.

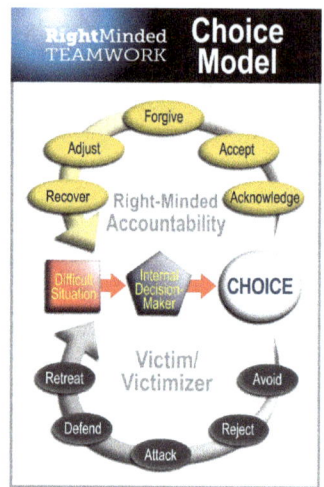

Reason is that part of your mind that always speaks for the Right Choice Attitudes & Behaviors. When you are facing a difficult team situation and need a **moment of Reason**, to find the best way to respond to a difficult team situation, say to yourself:

> *I am here to be truly helpful.*
>
> *I am here to represent Reason who sent me.*
>
> *I do not have to worry about what to say or what to do because Reason who sent me will direct me.*

As you pause, you are able to remember two Right-Minded responses, both of which are likely part of your Work Agreements:
- Engage in helpful problem-solving communication.
- Correct mistakes rather than punish and blame.

As you reflect while holding these two choices in your mind and heart, *intuitive* answers come to your "right" mind. Now that you have received Reason's advice, in a calm, "do-no-harm-work-as-one" voice, you say,

> *Here's a suggestion. Let's discuss what we know, the facts, about what happened. Then let's find an immediate solution.*
>
> *After we resolve the mistake, let's have a second team discussion, not to blame, but to create a Work Agreement so that this mistake doesn't happen again. How does that sound?*

If you had followed Ego's advice and continued your **avoidance behavior**, the conflict would have continued.

Since you chose to look towards Reason, you created an environment where you and your teammates **recovered** from the mistake, the **final step in the upper loop** of the model.

Reason, as always, has brought you - and hopefully everyone else, too - **back into your Right Mind.**

By listening to Reason, trusting your intuition, and following your **Work Agreements**, you train your mind to consistently return to the Unified Circle of Right-Minded Thinking.

What Does It Mean to "Train Your Mind?"

When your mind is well-trained, and a difficult team situation happens, you immediately stop for a moment of Reason. You remember your Work Agreements, and you consciously choose to follow them.

> *Training your mind simply means practicing your team's* **Work Agreements**, *and your psychological goals, especially during difficult team situations.*

By actively asking the question, "How did I **create**, **promote**, or **allow** this difficult situation to happen?" and then **stepping back in your mind** to listen for the answers, you will learn to hear and implicitly trust Reason's voice. Over time, this practice *shifts your perception* to finding solutions, allowing you *to hear the best answers* to the questions you ask. Once you know how to tune in to Reason to receive those answers, you will always know how to behave and respond.

So, how do you know when you are really hearing the voice of Reason and not Ego?

Firstly, answers from Reason will bring you a feeling of *inner peace* and *confidence*. Secondly, you will know you've heard Reason when *the answer you have received heals and resolves the difficulty* you face *while doing no harm* to anyone.

If your solution meets both of these criteria, rest assured you are listening to Reason. Over time, as you train your mind, it will become easier and easier for you to forgive the errors and mistakes of yourself and your teammates. You will simply recognize them, accept them, and immediately move toward finding solutions.

The Constantly Complaining Teammate (CCT)

Here's an example of how to **successfully train your mind**.

Think about a team experience where you've had to deal with a "CCT" - a Constantly Complaining Teammate.

In your mind, what do you picture when you see and interact with this person?

If what you see in your mind's eye is a big angry dog, ready to attack you and others, you are seeing the CCT through your Ego's eyes. You believe they are to be feared and avoided.

It is the perspective of an untrained and unforgiving mind. But it doesn't have to stay that way.

Alternatively, you can choose to follow Reason. When you genuinely desire to follow Reason's guidance, and you practice being mindful of your thoughts and choices, your perspective changes.

With Reason's help, instead of seeing your CCT as a vicious dog ready to attack, your new perception now shows you a cute-though-angry puppy. It is now *impossible* to fear them, and there is certainly no valid reason to avoid them.

With your new and healed perspective, you reinterpret the CCT's complaints as mistakes that need correction, not punishment. You accept their complaints as *their call for help*, not an attack.

Instead of reacting negatively, you say to yourself:

I will do my best to forgive this person for their constantly complaining behavior because I honestly think they care about doing a good job, even if they communicate poorly.

I will listen to their complaints. I'll ask clarifying questions to be sure I fully understand.

I will be kind, compassionate, non-judgmental, and civil in the way I respond. I will not get defensive. I will do no harm. I'll ask how we should resolve the situation.

When this Right-Minded perception shift happens, you will finally see your CCT for who they really are.

> *Rather than a person to be feared, avoided, harmed, or dismissed, your teammate is now a worthy sister or brother who wants to be heard, included, and helped – by YOU.*

They truly deserve no less than your Right-Minded, caring, and loving response.

Right-Minded Teamwork Attitudes & Behaviors

Thoughts and attitudes always precede teamwork behavior.

Right-Minded attitudes come from Reason. Wrong-minded attitudes come from Ego. The good news is that Right-Minded attitudes are natural. They are already inside you and your teammates.

When you think about any of the wrong-minded Ego attitudes listed below, ask yourself,

> *Was I born with these depressing, debilitating, and awful attitudes?*

Your answer will always be "no!" You learned those wrong-minded attitudes from Ego. That means **you can unlearn them, too.**

You *Can* Change Your Mind

In my years of team-building facilitation, I heard too many well-intentioned albeit wrong-minded teammates say,

> *That's just the way I am. I can't change.*

That is **simply not true**.

What is true is that they refused to change their minds.

> *When someone says they cannot change, what they are really saying is their behavior is more powerful than their mind.*

When they realize and joyfully accept **that their mind is in charge**, they have opened the way for happiness, inner peace, and Right-Minded Teamwork.

Why You Want to Change Your Perspective

Fixed perspectives prevent you from achieving Right-Minded Teamwork. Your limiting beliefs, interpretations, and lessons from Ego are blocks to Right-Minded Thinking.

To remove those blocks, you must transform your self-limiting thoughts. The first of RMT's 7 Mindfulness Training Lessons will help you do that.

Lesson one of the 7 Mindfulness Training Lessons states, *"I am never upset for the reason I think."*

Reminding yourself of this truth when you or your teammates are out of your Right mind will help you experience a **moment of Reason**. Instead of seeing your teammate's behavior as a negative Ego attack, you are able to reinterpret their behavior as a desperate **call for help** from you and your teammates.

With this new insight, you are able to respond to your teammate with Reason's wise guidance. With Reason's help, you have effectively changed your perspective.

. . . . .

Over decades of team-building work, I worked with hundreds of teams. Along the way, I collected their Right-Minded attitudes and behaviors into a list of choices that I grouped into **work behaviors** and **work processes**. The 30 Right-Minded Teamwork Attitudes & Behaviors starting on the next page will help you and your team change your perspective and achieve Right-Minded Thinking.

Work Behavior Attitudes

As the Decision-Maker, You Behave One Way or the Other!

EGO — DECISION MAKER — REASON

Demonstrate adversarial competition and power struggles	Demonstrate collaborative competition and synergy
Demonstrate victim or victimizer attitudes & behaviors	Exhibit accountable and responsible attitudes & behavior
Worry that "I am my mistakes;" continue to obsess over mistakes	Embrace that "I am not my mistakes;" mistakes are opportunities for me to learn
Noticeable lack of emotional maturity and empathy	Desire to be emotionally mature and compassionate
Exhibit self-centered attitudes	Exhibit we-centered attitudes
Hold & project grievances; Never forget or forgive	Embrace & extend forgiveness; Let go of issues from the past
After mistakes, helplessness occurs, and I choose to give up or not try as hard	After mistakes, forgiveness occurs, and I choose to try again and again

Work Behavior Attitudes (Continued)

There's a mindset of scarcity, a belief that to give is to lose	There's an attitude of abundance, a belief that to give is to receive
There is suspicion, closed-mindedness, and resistance to change	There is readiness and open-mindedness for positive change
Too often, people restate their position, believing they are right, and others are wrong	We always seek mutual understanding: believing together, we are right
I believe I'm the smartest, and I can prove it	We believe none of us is as smart as all of us
I demonstrate a conscious or unconscious attitude of confusion, chaos, complexity, and drama	We continually demonstrate a conscious attitude of clarity, order, simplicity, and calmness
There's a widespread belief that difficult team situations and changes determine how we feel	We know for sure that our minds determine how we feel about difficult situations or changes
We believe it is best to keep quiet when correction is needed	We have a team culture of appropriately speaking up when a correction is needed
We believe in these attitudes: vulnerability, unkindness, hate, attack, blame	We embrace these attitudes: invulnerability, love, kindness, do no harm, work as one

Work Behavior Attitudes (Continued)

We believe in power over others	We believe in power with others
Growth is painful; remember, if there is no pain, there is no gain	Growth doesn't have to be painful; learning is joyously attained and gladly remembered
It is best to do unto others (reject, attack, defend) before they do unto you	We do unto others (accept, forgive, adjust) as we would have them do unto us
There is a feeling of avoidance and criticism among teammates	There is a spirit of acknowledgment and reward among teammates
There is a love and a need for power, fame, money, and pleasure	We strive for non-attachment to power, fame, money, and pleasure
Our team is a battleground where conflict is prolonged as we act like victims or victimizers	Our team is our learning classroom where conflict is resolved as we act like Right-Minded Teammates
There is mistrust, fear, and lack of safety among teammates	There is trust, peace, and safety among teammates
Defensiveness is prevalent in our team	Defenselessness is widespread in our team

Process Behavior Attitudes

Your Team Can Operate One Way or the Other!

The team's purpose, vision, and mission are unclear and not supported	Our team continuously clarifies our purpose, vision, and mission and actively supports them
There is no discernable team operating system	There is an efficient, continuous improvement team operating system in place
There is a predominant attitude of avoidance and complaining	We have an attitude and a system for acknowledgment and reward
Disagreements and a lack of clear roles and responsibilities exist	We periodically clarify teammate roles and responsibilities
We are unclear who makes decisions and how	Our team has a clear and effective decision-making Work Agreement
We spend too much time and energy applying inefficient work processes	Our work processes and procedures are clear, understood, accepted, and efficient
Too often, people are punished for making mistakes	We always embrace an attitude of converting mistakes into learning opportunities

Actionable Attitudes = Better Behaviors

These Right-Minded attitudes are practical. However, these noble thoughts and attitudes will do no good unless you discuss them and define what they mean for your team.

Once you have identified and defined the behaviors associated with your chosen attitudes, captured in your team Work Agreements, you must also make the conscious choice to live them going forward.

Don't let your team's insignificant, Ego-driven squabbles pull you down.

Be vigilant and demonstrate by your actions and behaviors that you have risen above your old, petty, teamwork battleground issues.

No team situation can pull you into Ego's realm of conflict when you believe it is far better to collaborate and win than argue and lose.

Remember, it is from your collective Right Mind that you create your Work Agreements. And when you make and follow your promises, you are uniting with each other without the Ego. When you do that, you have returned to the United Circle of Right-Minded Thinking. From that unified circle, it will be much easier to recover from any difficult team situation because you have, at that moment, restored your team's collective Right Mind to Reason.

Return to the Unified Circle of Right-Minded Thinking

When your team discusses and agrees on your psychological goals – your consciously chosen set of attitudes and behaviors as described in your Work Agreements – you have created your team's collective thought system.

By uniting with each other in this way and openly committing to one another through your Work Agreements, you are renouncing Ego in yourself and your teammates and collectively committing to train your minds to follow Reason.

This process of creating team Work Agreements is your undivided declaration of interdependence. Together, you and your teammates are asserting,

> *We hold these mindful truths to be self-evident, that all minds are created equal, and whosoever believes it will have everlasting freedom to choose Right-Minded Teamwork.*

Your declaration, combined with your daily acts of living your team Work Agreements, is your return to the forgiving Unified Circle of Right-Minded Thinking.

So, who will you follow? Every day, the choice is yours.

> *Follow Reason, and declare your freedom from Ego's battlefields.*

> *Follow Reason, and join others who believe Right-Minded thoughts are self-evident and true.*

> *Follow Reason, and transform fixed perspectives. Reinterpret attack behaviors as a call for help – your help.*

*Follow Reason, and your team will agree on a Right-Minded set of attitudes and behaviors as described in your **Work Agreements.***

*Follow **Reason** and your **Work Agreements**, and renounce Ego while uniting with your fellow teammates.*

Follow Reason, and return to your ultimate goal, the forgiving Unified Circle of Right-Minded Thinking.

Who Will You Listen To?

As the Decision-Maker, the kind of experience you have in life and within your team is a direct result of your attitudes and behaviors. Here is a story to illustrate.

Once upon a time, a wise and loving grandparent was teaching their grandchild about life. Referencing the battle between Ego and Reason, the grandparent said, *"A fight is going on inside of me, and it is a terrible fight. It is between two wolves. One wolf represents feelings like fear, anger, guilt, arrogance, and sin. The other wolf represents feelings like trust, gentleness, defenselessness, and open-mindedness."*

Pausing a moment, the grandparent added, *"The same fight is going on inside of you and inside all human beings."*

After thinking about it for a minute or two, the grandchild asked, *"Which wolf will win?"*

The grandparent leaned forward and whispered, *"The one you feed."*

Puppeteer & Puppet

Another beautiful way to think about and embrace "you" as the Decision-Maker is to relate the real you to a puppet show. In this example, the Decision-Maker is the puppeteer, the one "behind the curtain," inside your mind.

Your attitudes and behaviors are your puppets. They are selected by your Decision-Maker and seen and heard by others as you demonstrate them daily "on stage" (as you go through your life). You control these puppets, these attitudes and behaviors, because you are the puppeteer, the Decision-Maker.

> **RIGHT-MINDED Accountability**
> is the **desire, willingness,** and **ability** to change my mind & behavior in order to effectively respond to difficult situations.
>
> **This means owning my part in the situation by asking:**
>
> *"How did I CREATE, PROMOTE, or ALLOW this difficult situation to happen?"*
>
> RightMindedTeamwork.com

When you face difficult situations, it's critical to remember this truth and take control of your mind. When you remember who you are, you can consciously direct your attitudes and behaviors in an accountable, responsible, Right-Minded way.

By taking control of your mind, you strengthen your:

> ...*desire,* **willingness**, *and* **ability** *to change your attitude and behavior to find a healthier way to respond to your difficult situation.*

Taking control of your mind, which can happen instantly, leads you to a mature and practical way of thinking and questioning.

That means you:

> *...accept and own your part in the difficult situation by asking yourself, "How did I **create**, **promote**, or **allow** this situation to occur with my attitudes and behaviors?"*

It is easier to change your attitude and behavior when you consciously recognize and own your part as the puppeteer. You know you have the power to mitigate and possibly eliminate the problematic situation.

You Are the King & Queen

Here is one more way of thinking and describing you, the Decision-Maker. Imagine yourself as the king or queen of your kingdom.

Now, also imagine a problematic situation that arises as two warring tribes vie for your royal attention.

These warring tribes are your inner thoughts. They are very real to you, just like your dreams at night seem real until you awaken. These inner thoughts come from years of living and being programmed to value various life principles.

One tribe, led by Ego-based thoughts, loudly argues their case to you. They have come asking for your support, presenting themselves either as victims of the situation or as victimizers who believe you should help them launch a counterattack. This group's motto is, *"It wasn't my fault! You need to fix it and protect me."*

The other tribe, led by Reason, is not really interested in a war. Instead, Reason quietly offers win-win options that will heal and resolve the situation. Reason's tribe's motto is, *"I am not a victim of the world I see. I am here to be truly helpful."*

As the king or queen, once you have heard both sides, it is up to you to choose how you will respond to this difficult situation. Will you start an Ego-fueled war? Or will you be Right-Minded and accountable?

The choice is always yours.

What Attitudes Are You Feeding?

So, which wolf are you feeding? Which puppets are you choosing? As king or queen, which tribe are you listening to? The costs and benefits are clear.

If you want to transform any difficult situation, your Decision-Maker must first acknowledge your own role by asking, ***"What am I doing that is creating, promoting, or allowing this situation to persist?"***

Exploring the answers to this question will help you feed the Right-Minded tribe inside you, leading you to the best solutions for all concerned.

The 10 Characteristics of Right-Minded Teammates

Right-Minded Teammates have diverse backgrounds, vastly different experiences, and display a wide range of skills. No two are alike. Still, there are certain characteristics all Right-Minded Teammates share.

These characteristics align the teammate's authentic self with the RMT motto of *Do no harm and work as one*. They are:

1. Trust
2. Honesty
3. Tolerance
4. Gentleness
5. Joy
6. Defenselessness
7. Generosity
8. Patience
9. Open-mindedness
10. Faithfulness

When you help your team create and live team Work Agreements, they will be well on their way to living these characteristics.

How does the Right-Minded Teammate live these characteristics?

They do two things when difficult situations occur.

First, they remind themselves of their commitment to *thinking* in a do-no-harm way. Second, they choose to demonstrate do-no-harm *behaviors* that align with their Right-Minded attitudes, such as finding solutions to challenging situations.

It is not always easy to do these two things, but it is always that simple.

To encourage your team to embrace and live these Right-Minded characteristics, check out these two RMT books:

7 Mindfulness Training Lessons: *Improve Teammates' Ability to Work as One with Right-Minded Thinking* will teach you how to apply RMT's seven, powerful thinking lessons to encourage Right-Minded, unified teamwork.

How to Apply the Right Choice Model: *Create a Right-Minded Team That Works as One* teaches you how to transform a disappointed team customer into a 100% satisfied customer by making Right-Minded choices, all of which align with the above list of characteristics.

For now, though, let's take a closer look at each of these 10, Right-Minded Teammate characteristics.

1. Trust

Trust is the foundational characteristic for teammates who desire to create and sustain Right-Minded Teamwork. Right-Minded Teammates trust one another because their own past experience has taught them that, in all situations, a forgiving attitude creates safety for teammates to collaborate and resolve difficulties.

2. Honesty

For the Right-Minded Teammate, honesty means more than just telling the truth. It refers to consistency in thought and deed. An honest, Right-Minded Teammate is consistently looking within and striving to align thoughts, words, and behaviors with the team's psychological goals and forgiving values. This kind of honesty is essential to creating and sustaining Right-Minded Teamwork.

3. Tolerance

Judgment is the opposite of forgiveness; it implies a lack of trust. Tolerance indicates non-judgment. Tolerant teammates do not judge one another because they know that though they are not the same, all Right-Minded Teammates are equal. Their tolerance creates space for the wisdom of diversity to surface, and their equality allows them to work together as one.

4. Gentleness

Right-Minded Teammates believe that gentleness is the only sane response to challenging situations and circumstances. Whereas harshness and judgment close doors, gentleness opens them. With gentleness, it is easy for teammates to do no harm as they work as one – with teammates and customers alike.

5. Joy

Joy is the inevitable result for Right-Minded teammates who are gentle and non-judgmental. Fear is impossible for those who are gentle, especially during challenging situations. Joy comes from gentleness, tolerance, honesty, and forgiveness.

6. Defenselessness

Right-Minded Teammates understand that defenses are foolish, judgmental attitudes and behaviors that prevent the team from finding solutions to difficult situations. When teammates summon the courage to forgive and trust themselves and to look honestly at their wrong-minded defenses without judgment, they can lay those debilitating arguments gently aside, creating the proper conditions for honestly doing no harm and working as one.

7. Generosity

Right-Minded Teammates honestly and humbly give all they know to help their team create Right-Minded Teamwork and achieve 100% customer satisfaction. The world teaches that if you give something away, you lose it, but Right-Minded Teammates realize that to give *is* to receive. They eagerly participate with their teammates to create solutions to solve challenging situations, bringing joy and satisfaction to the team through their gentle generosity.

8. Patience

Teammates who know Right-Minded Teamwork is the outcome they want can easily afford to wait without concern. Because their goal is to be tolerant and gentle with their teammates, patience comes naturally. The highest desire is to work as one.

9. Open-Mindedness

Judgment, or wrong-mindedness, closes teammates' minds, creating resistance to Right-Minded Teamwork. To ensure they do no harm while working as one, Right-Minded Teammates embrace open-mindedness, also known as Right-Mindedness.

10. Faithfulness

Faithfulness describes a teammate's trust in their team's version of Right-Minded Teamwork. When a teammate is faithful, they effortlessly and wholeheartedly believe in Right-Minded Teamwork. They *want* to do no harm and work as one. They know none of us is as smart as all of us. When applied during challenging circumstances, their faithfulness inevitably leads the team to happy outcomes.

How Does a Team Use the Right Choice Model?

There are three possible ways to integrate the Right Choice Model into your team.

You can present and discuss the Right Choice Model in a:
- team meeting
- team problem-resolving meeting
- team-building workshop

Present & Discuss Right Choice in a Team Meeting

The team leader prints and distributes the Right Choice poster and Right Choice cards to all teammates. These materials contain all the key steps, words, and concepts for teaching Right Choice.

Printing the posters and cards is easy. Reminder: To download RMT models and materials to give teammates, go to RightMindedTeamwork.com, and search for this book's companion **Reusable Resources & Templates**.

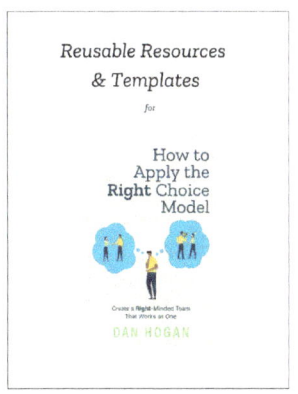

To begin the meeting, the team leader describes victim behaviors and accountable behaviors, comparing and contrasting Right-Minded, accountable behavior (the upper loop of the Right Choice Model) to the wrong-minded, victim behavior (the lower loop).

After a short discussion, the leader asks:

> *"Do we all agree that we want to function as Right-Minded teammates?"*

Everyone will say:

> *Of course, we need to approach our challenging situation in a Right-Minded, accountable way. Let's get started.*

The team's agreement has established their intention to act as Right-Minded teammates.

 ***To Learn More…***

Prefer to learn by ***video***?

Watch a step-by-step video on applying the Right Choice Model and its team-changing concepts. Go to RightMindedTeamwork.com, search for the book ***How to Apply the Right Choice Model*** and look for the instructional video on the book's description page titled, *"Right Choice Cards & Right Choice Behavior."*

Present & Discuss Right Choice in a Team Problem-Resolution Meeting

The second option for presenting Right Choice is quite similar to option one, but it uses a recent, difficult team situation to underscore the benefit of choosing Right-Minded behaviors.

Here's an example to illustrate. Let's say your team's primary customer just let you know they were very disappointed in your product or service quality. Your poor or marginal quality has cost them time and money, forcing them to wait for their product. Your team's reputation is now on the line.

As the team leader, you decide the best way to address and resolve your unhappy customer's issue is to conduct an all-hands, problem-resolution meeting.

At the beginning, you present the Right Choice Model by incorporating the customer's concerns, saying something like,

> *We have a difficult situation. It can be resolved if we accept responsibility and forgive ourselves for what happened. If we truly do that, we will create the right frame of mind to adjust our work behavior and practices and recover from this situation.*
>
> *Our only other choice is to reject, attack, or try to defend our team. If we do that, we will be in the wrong frame of mind, and we will not resolve this problem.*

Shall we all commit to demonstrating Right-Minded and accountable behaviors in today's meeting so we can successfully recover and regain our customers' trust?

Everyone agrees to resolve the problem through forgiveness, not blame.

Next, you invite the team to honestly ask themselves, *"What have we done to **create**, **promote** or **allow** our customers' dissatisfaction?"* Asking this question helps the team uncover dysfunctional teamwork behaviors and convert them into actionable resolutions. These team commitments are captured in a team Work Agreement.

Next, you share your new Work Agreement(s) with the customer, illustrating your commitment to improvement. They believe that if you truly follow the Agreement(s), they will be happy and satisfied with your product or service.

As a team, when you follow your Work Agreements, you increase the likelihood of regaining your customers' confidence and trust. As you begin meeting or exceeding your customers' expectations, you win as a team, and your customers benefit, too. Your team's recovery can be traced back, at least in part, to your collective choice to follow your Work Agreements and to act and behave in a Right-Minded way.

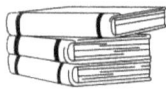 *To Learn More…*

For more about presenting and discussing the Right Choice Model in a team problem-resolution meeting, see the upcoming section entitled ***How to Present & Apply the Right Choice Model in My Team.***

Present & Discuss the Right Choice Model in a Team-Building Workshop

The third for presenting the Right Choice Model includes everything in the first two options and also uses teammate information gathered by a facilitator in private interviews. As in option two, this option advocates that teammates create team Work Agreements that align with their agreed-upon Right choices.

Executing this option leverages these three RMT methods:
- 5 Elements of Right-Minded Teamwork
- 5 Elements 90-Day Implementation Plan
- 12 Steps for Designing an RMT Workshop

5 Elements of Right-Minded Teamwork

- The ideal RMT implementation plan includes three team-building workshops. These workshops are best organized and guided by a team-building facilitator.

- The Right Choice Model is presented in the first workshop.

- During the first workshop, the team creates several Work Agreements. Work Agreements are one of the 5 Elements.

- Afterward, teammates use their Work Agreements to resolve their current challenging teamwork situations.

RMT's 5 Elements Implementation Plan

What is the best way to apply RMT in your team? There is no one answer to this question. However, the three-workshop plan presented here has proven effective countless times.

First Workshop – Work Agreements
- Present the Right Choice Model
- Identify team psychological goals and values (Element #2)
- Create at least one team Work Agreement (Element #3)
- Identify two or three improvement projects for the next 90 days

Second Workshop – Operating System
- Reset and reaffirm business goals (Element #1) and agree on the Team Operating System (Element #4)

Third Workshop - Teammates
- Conduct a Right-Minded Teammate development workshop (Element #5).

90-Day Operating Plan - Ongoing
- Every 90 days, conduct another Team Performance Factor Assessment, and then the team meets to assess progress, identify opportunities, take action, and achieve new teamwork improvements.

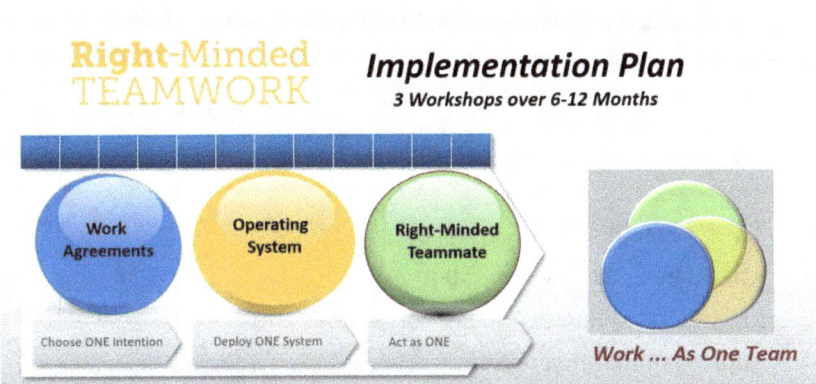

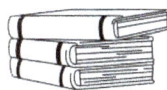 *To Learn More…*

To learn more about the **5 Elements of Right-Minded Teamwork** and the **three workshop Implementation Plan**, visit your favorite book retailer or RightMindedTeamwork.com, and pick up your copy of *Right-Minded Teamwork in Any Team*: The *Ultimate Team Building Method to Create a Team That Works as One.*

12 Steps: How to Design a
Right-Minded, Team-Building Workshop

- The 12-step process is a thorough, real-world, team-building approach.

- The facilitator conducts teammate interviews in **Step 7** to gather teammates' ideas for improving their teamwork.

- The teammates' ideas are summarized in a Punch List. All teammates receive a copy. In time, all Punch List items are addressed and resolved in team-building workshops.

- Each Right-Minded team-building workshop will seek to resolve several desired outcomes.

In these two books, ***How to Facilitate Team Work Agreements*** and ***Design a Right-Minded, Team-Building Workshop***: *12 Steps to Create a Team That Works as One,* you will see two outcomes from a real client team.

When you read these books, you will quickly see the effectiveness of this workshop-based approach for applying the Right Choice Model in your team.

A Real Team Workshop Story

Synopsis

Without strong internal processes and teammate trust, teams fall apart.

Such was the experience of Peter and Randy, co-project managers of an 85-person major capital project team. This team was responsible for designing and building a billion-dollar chemical plant.

Twenty-five teammates were from the client organization, which owned the plant. The 60 other teammates were from an international engineering company. All 85 teammates were located in the same office.

Team members constantly disagreed over work processes, and toxic interpersonal relationships caused additional stress and dysfunction.

After conducting teammate interviews, I learned many teammates had complaints about the number of required team meetings. They felt meetings were ineffective and not valuable. We decided this was the issue to address in the first workshop.

First Workshop

Before discussing how to improve meetings, I briefly presented the Right Choice Model. Then I said,

> *You just agreed you're ready to improve meetings.*
>
> *After having interviewed all of you, it's my view that this outcome is very achievable if you remain committed to discussing them in a responsible, Right-Minded way.*

What that means is that you are willing, as individuals and as a team, to ask yourselves, "How did we create, promote or allow this situation to happen?

Your answers will lead you to solutions. And those solutions will be captured in your first team Work Agreement.

We will also use your Agreement to address and resolve the other issues on your Punch List. We won't get to all of those in today's workshop, but we will in future workshops.

Is everyone willing to live and follow your Right Choice attitudes and behaviors?"

Everyone agreed.

They created a Work Agreement that mapped out how they would use agendas, identified desired outcomes, and laid ground rules to keep meetings on track in two hours. They also addressed how to speak up if a meeting discussion went sideways. By the end of the workshop, they had a plan forward.

Results

After just one month of living their new Work Agreement, teammates reported getting more work done because they were not in so many meetings. The meetings they did have were more productive, organized, and better facilitated.

The team declared the meeting Work Agreement a success, and managers Randy and Peter estimated they were able to **save $10,000 a week in labor costs.** Their story demonstrates the profitability of Right Choice's central philosophy and motto: Do no harm, and work as one.

Right Choice & Your Team Work Agreements

In this book's preface, I shared the following RMT definition:

> *Right-Minded Teamwork is a business-oriented, psychological approach to team building where **acceptance**, **forgiveness**, and **adjustment** are teammate characteristics, and 100% customer satisfaction is the team's result.*

When you apply RMT, you create Work Agreements that describe your team's behavioral characteristics of **acceptance**, **forgiveness**, and **adjustment**. Those descriptions *are* your team's Right Choices. Your Work Agreements also define your team's psychological approach to teamwork. They *are* a written version of your team's thought system.

A team without Work Agreements is like a machine without an operator's manual. Teammates might function at acceptable levels for a while, but eventually, they will decline into separateness and egotistical self-interest.

A Work Agreement is a covenant, promise, or pledge that transforms dysfunctional and non-productive work behavior. It is not a ground rule. It is an emotionally mature promise based on collaboration and achieving customer satisfaction. Emotionally mature and productive teammates create Work Agreements that sustain Right-Minded Teamwork because they have experienced the benefits of a unified team with shared interests and common goals. They choose to follow Reason, not Ego.

Creating Work Agreements

Since you have been in many teams, you know it is not a matter of if conflict will occur among teammates. It is a question of when.

For that reason, it is far better to have Work Agreements in place before disagreements happen. Your existing Work Agreements will serve to mitigate and even make positive use of those clashes when they occur. However, even if your team is already in conflict, it's still not and will never be too late to create and live team Work Agreements.

In the book *How to Facilitate Team Work Agreements: A Practical, 10-Step Process for Building a Right-Minded Team That Works as One,* you will learn the fundamental principles for creating and facilitating Work Agreements. These steps will ensure you move your teammates into their collective Right Minds,  which guarantees they make practical, powerful Work Agreements.

Two Types of Work Agreements

Almost all teamwork issues can be resolved with Work Agreements. Two types of Agreements capture your team's Right Choices.

1. A **process Work Agreement** describes who does what and which work methods they use.

2. A **behavioral Work Agreement** describes how people will behave while they perform their tasks.

Process Agreements define work tasks in terms of roles, responsibilities, interfaces, or procedures.

Behavioral Agreements highlight, with transparency, the ways teammates *choose to* bring to light, communicate, and resolve difficult performance issues or interpersonal conflicts.

Work Agreement Structure

A Work Agreement that is wholeheartedly agreed upon includes a **Team Choice** or **Intention Statement** that defines your choice followed by **Clarifications or Conditions for Acceptance**.

Intention:
1. Each teammate will communicate their thoughts and feelings in appropriate ways.

Clarifications or Conditions:
A. We follow the spirit and intent of our company values.
B. If we believe another person is communicating inappropriately, we will call it to their attention in private.
C. Even though this Agreement addresses inappropriate communication behaviors, we also agree to give positive teammate reinforcement when we see and hear excellent communication.

Real Team Work Agreements

Below you will find two real examples of Work Agreements. The first one is a behavioral team communication Work Agreement. The other is a process Work Agreement around decision-making.

I worked with these teams for a few years. These were phenomenally successful Work Agreements because teammates passionately created and actively ***lived their Right Choices*** day in and day out.

Behavioral Agreement – Communication

Team Choice: Intention Statement
1. Each teammate will communicate in a respectful way.

Clarifications / Conditions for Acceptance:

A. We will use good communication techniques that include appropriate body language and tone of voice, plus suitable words.
B. If we see or hear disrespect or we hear an inappropriate behind-the-back conversation, we own it and need to step in.
C. If someone unintentionally shows disrespect, we will give them the benefit of the doubt, let them know, and create a new way to interact going forward.
D. We will actively support team decisions in word, deed, and energy; we will use our decision-making protocol agreement for key decisions.
E. We will be on time for meetings.
F. We will ask, "May I interrupt you?"
G. We will use observable facts during disagreements and decision-making, and we will acknowledge when we are using assumptions.
H. We will understand each other's roles, ask for help if we need it, share relevant information and if helpful, give constructive feedback in private.
I. If someone continues to break this agreement, we will tell them that we will invite a third party to help if there is continued disagreement. If that doesn't solve the issues, we will all go to a higher authority for support and resolution.

Process Agreement – Decision-Making Protocol

Team Choice: Intention Statement
2. We will go for consensus for all key team decisions, but our fallback will be that Maria [team leader] will decide if we cannot reach a consensus.

Conditions for Acceptance / Clarification
A. Before entering a discussion, we'll agree on the decision-making method and fall back, plus when [date] a decision will be made.
B. Before delving into a solution, we will create an opportunity or problem statement.
C. At the beginning of our discussion, we will determine boundaries & givens (i.e., time sensitivity; cost, hassle, impact, 80% or 100% perfect decision, etc.).
D. We provide a business case (appropriate justification) for our decision, including cost/benefit.
E. During our conversations, we will advocate and inquire. We will not hold back. For instance, we will acknowledge assumptions and facts.
F. To create the best solutions, we will also think about alternative ways to test our solution (Devil's Advocate).
G. If we find ourselves at an impasse, we will call a "time out" to calm down or acquire more technical information.
H. When a decision is made, we will accurately represent and support the decision.
I. We do this agreement because we want to improve teamwork and trust in one another.
J. We will hold ourselves and others accountable for living the letter and the spirit of this agreement; we will fine-tune it as necessary
---

With my guidance, it took this 10-person team about four hours to create these two Work Agreements. Use your imagination as to what they said to each other that made these successful Agreements.

Onboarding New Teammates

When a new leader or teammate joins your team, it is vitally important to properly onboard them within their first week on the job. In a single short meeting where everyone attends, the onboarding is easily and effectively accomplished. Present all your RMT goals and Work Agreements along with why they were created. Give them a chance to ask you clarifying questions. Afterward, you ask them to accept the team's goals and actively live their Right Choices as described in your Work Agreements.

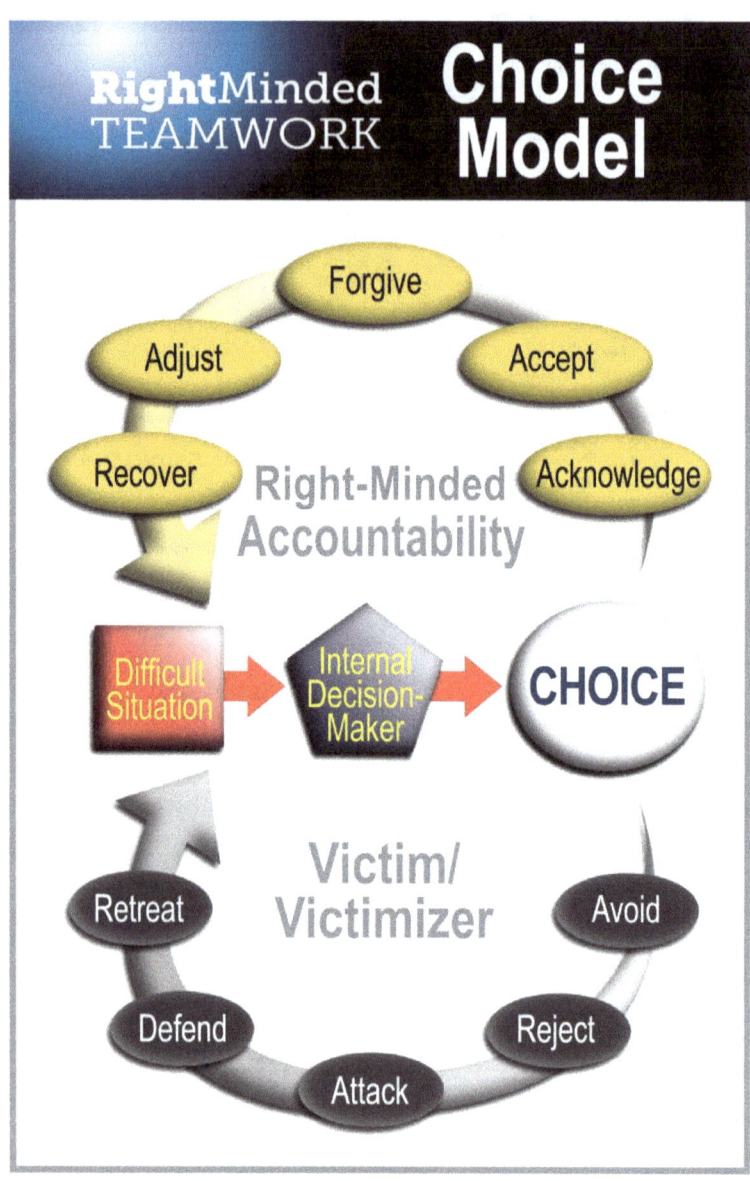

Right Choice as a Personal Tool

Let's take a closer look at how you, personally, would apply the Right Choice Model to a difficult team situation that is happening to you.

First, let's define accountability, which is a virtual synonym of Right Choice.

Accountability: A Definition

There are many definitions of accountability. For Right Choice and Right-Minded Teamwork purposes, we will use the one included on the Right Choice card. It states:

Right-Minded accountability is the desire, willingness, and ability to change my mind and behavior in order to effectively respond to difficult situations.

That means I own my part in the situation by asking and answering this question:

How did I create, promote, or allow this difficult situation to happen?

Simply by asking yourself this question, you are already moving into a Right-Minded mindset. As you will see in the step-by-step explanation below, you will never ask yourself this question as a victim or victimizer.

In every circumstance, and especially during difficult team situations, Right-Minded Teammates practice mindfulness to move them into a Right-Minded, ally-focused way of thinking and behaving.

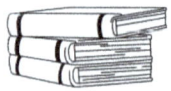 ***To Learn More…***

For more on practicing mindfulness the RMT way, check out the RMT book, *7 **Mindfulness Training Lessons***: *Improve Teammates' Ability to Work as One with Right-Minded Thinking*.

Go to RightMindedTeamwork.com or visit your favorite book retailer and pick up your copy of *7 **Mindfulness Training Lessons.***

Right Choice:
Step-by-Step Application

In life and in business, both positive and negative events happen. They happen to individuals, teams, families, and organizations.

We cannot always control what happens to us, but we can control how we respond to each situation.

High-performing individuals and teams recognize the importance of responding to events in a responsible way rather than getting caught in the trap of feeling and acting like a victim.

The Right Choice Model helps you answer these questions:

- What does accountability look like in my team and in me?
- What's the best way for me to hold others accountable?
- How do I know if I'm accountable?

Facing a Difficult Team Situation

Here is a work scenario you have likely experienced: A teammate is not pulling their weight and is not performing their job very well.

To see how the Right Choice Model applies, we will first look at the wrong-minded choice path, the one to avoid. Then, I will explain the transition step, and we will end with how to follow the Right-Minded choice path.

Avoid

When you choose the victim path, the first thing you will do is try to avoid the teammate and their poor performance.

Before you feel guilty, rest assured we've all done this in the past. It's okay and even healthy to admit it. The good news is you are now committed to not avoiding such situations anymore.

However, to become more aware of this Ego-inspired response, we need to look at our behavior honestly. Only then can we unlearn them and let them go! So, before we head down the Right Choice path, let's trek through the lower loop of the Right Choice Model. We'll get to the good stuff in the upper loop in a minute.

No one else is saying anything to the teammate, either. You think by avoiding the problem, maybe the situation will just go away by itself. You hope the leader will see the poor performance and either address the teammate or terminate them.

When you demonstrate avoidance behavior like this, does the teammate's poor performance get better on its own? No, of course not.

Eventually, the teammate's poor performance will be noticed by most of your teammates.

At that point, you must all stop pretending you don't see what's happening.

Reject

Once on the wrong-minded choice path, your next choice will be to deny or reject the situation by telling yourself that the teammate's poor performance isn't that big of a problem.

You decide you can still do your job just fine by working around that teammate... even though the situation is beginning to irritate you and a few others.

When you reject a situation like this and ignore its impact on you, does the situation tend to get better? Again, no.

Since no one is addressing the teammate's poor performance, there will inevitably come a time when their behavior crosses the threshold from poor to unacceptable performance.

At that point, you will discover you can only do so much avoiding and rejecting.

Attack

Once your irritation has peaked, you easily escalate into the next victim behavior: attacking.

You might blame and attack the poorly performing teammate. You might attack other teammates, the team leader, or even your organization.

Does attacking others fix situations like this? Once more, the answer is no. Blaming and attacking steal your personal power, allowing others to imprison you.

Think about this carefully: When you blame others, following Ego into an Ego attack, what you are saying is that *your life cannot get better until the other person changes.* So, if the other person doesn't change, and you choose to keep on believing your life can't get better until they do, your only option is to remain bitter and angry, attacking them about the wrong they have caused you.

Your insistence on being the victim, suffering over their refusal to change, indicates that you believe they have more power over your mind than you do. But this is never really the case.

Eventually, with Reason's help, you'll teach yourself to use those Ego-centered thoughts as an inner alarm to help you move back into your Right Mind through a **moment of Reason**. But more on that in a minute.

Defend

Sooner or later, because you are attacking, others start attacking you.

For example, one of your teammates says to you,

Why didn't you bring our teammate's poor performance to our attention? We don't work with them very often, but you work with them every day! You're part of the problem. Why were you hiding this from us? What are you going to do about it? How will YOU fix it?

Now the tables have turned. You're being attacked for your poor performance, namely your **avoidance behavior**. You're offended. You start defending yourself.

Often, defending yourself gives you the delusional excuse that it is okay to do nothing. It helps you rationalize and convince yourself that somebody else is the problem. You conclude that you don't have to change your behavior at all. The other person should be required to change instead.

Your response might sound like this:

I'm not their supervisor. I should not have to be responsible for their performance. I have too much work to do, and I often have to redo YOUR work. So, don't blame me. This is not MY problem.

When teammates are stuck in attack-and-defend conversations, do they solve situations like this? No. Everything just gets worse.

Retreat

Let's face it. There is only so much attack and defend behavior a person can take. It's emotionally draining; the weight of constant judgment is exhausting.

At this stage of the lower loop of the Right Choice Model, you decide you must retreat or hide from this situation. That way, you can avoid it and not be given responsibility for fixing it.

Common retreat reactions include sending out "verbal missiles" to teammates during conversations or meetings such as, "If you'd gotten here earlier... you would have known the meeting time had been changed," or leaving the poor-performing teammate out. You might "forget" to include them in important meetings or critical projects. They may even be excluded from social functions such as going out together for lunch.

Most teammates know that if you retreat too long, you will attract negative attention. So, to help you deal with this situation, you might choose to become invisible or attempt to hide.

Hiding behavior is demonstrated in many ways. In our example situation, here are three things you might do or say to your teammates.

1. You claim you are too busy attending to some other crisis that you simply cannot be responsible for dealing with this poor-performing teammate. You simply don't have time, so others must deal with it.

2. You are unavailable or hard to find. Other teammates write you emails or leave voicemails, but you do not return their calls.

3. You demonstrate confusion even though you are anything but confused. You might say to teammates, "When you guys figure out who's supposed to do what, let me know, and I'll see if I can help. Again, this is not MY problem, and I'm not sure how it got this way."

Summarizing Wrong-Minded Choices

Have you dealt with the situation effectively when you respond by attacking, defending, retreating, or hiding?

No. Of course not!

When teammates are stuck in the wrong-minded victim conversations, the problem they were arguing about stays unresolved. And, to make matters worse, the next time you encounter a similar situation, you will cycle through these very same behaviors even faster, deepening the problem.

To solve the problem, you and your teammates must *choose again.*

You must move to the upper loop of the Right Choice Model, which is the Unified Circle of Right-Minded Thinking. You must avoid getting stuck in the lower loop, which is the divided circle of wrong-minded thinking.

You must stop and remember your team's Right Choice Work Agreements.

The instant you stop to genuinely find the right answers, you experience a transitional **moment of Reason**.

Was I Born with These Attitudes?

Before we explore this joyful transition step, do you remember the list of 30 attitudes & behaviors? After you reviewed them, I asked you to answer this question:

> *Was I born with these depressing, debilitating, and awful attitudes?*

You answered, "no, I was NOT!" You accepted the truth that you learned those wrong-minded attitudes from Ego.

That means *you can unlearn them, too*. The transition step in the middle of the Right Choice Model is how. Let's look at it now.

Moment of Reason:
Transitioning from Wrong to Right Choice

You must transition your mindset when you realize you and your teammates are stuck in an attack-and-defend conversation. To do so, look within, and ask yourself,

> *What am I doing to create, promote, or allow this blaming conversation to carry on?*

The moment you ask yourself that question and answer it, you are accepting that you were standing by and saying nothing. You were **avoiding**, which is the **first step in the wrong-minded choice cycle**.

Now, you change your mind.

You remember you committed to Right-Minded attitudes and behaviors in your team-building workshop, as described in your team's Right Choice Work Agreements.

Changing your mind was your **moment of Reason**.

You also remembered the questions the Right Choice facilitator posed to you and your teammates. The facilitator asked,

> *Do we desire to work in an environment where we rule our destiny or one that rules us?*
>
> *Do we desire a work environment where we are powerful instead of helpless?*
>
> *Do we desire a team environment with no enemies, only allies, and where our mistakes are corrected - not punished?*

When you answered, you realized you prefer working together in the Right Choice ways. You committed to living it from then on. Now, in your moment of Reason, you recommit. Instead of looking to blame, you are ready to acknowledge, accept, and own your part in this situation.

"We've already agreed how we were to address that issue, haven't we?"

I heard this exact question and witnessed the team's "moment of Reason" in their second RMT workshop. When the team realized they had created Work Agreements three months prior that addressed the exact same issue they were now re-arguing, they immediately shifted back into their collective Right Mind. Their moment of Reason brought them back to productive conflict resolution.

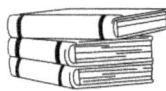 ***To Learn More…***

For the full story, check out the RMT book ***How to Facilitate Team Work Agreements:*** *A Practical, 10-Step Process for Building a Right-Minded Team That Works as One*, available at RightMindedTeamwork.com or your favorite book retailer. Look for the section *"Sustaining Team Work Agreements,"* and find the portion titled, *"We've already agreed on how we were to address that issue, haven't we?"*

Acknowledge

Let's go back to the situation where your teammate is not pulling their weight and look at it through a different lens.

Instead of ignoring or avoiding the situation, you acknowledge what's happening. You choose to respond responsibly.

Instead of hoping the situation will go away, you admit to yourself and other teammates that there is a problem that needs to be addressed.

You don't have an answer to that problem yet, but you are willing to discuss it with the teammate and other teammates in a non-judgmental manner.

Accept

The next step in Right Choice is to accept and "own your part" in the situation.

High-performing teams and individuals always ask themselves,

"How have I created, promoted, or allowed this situation to occur?"

This step is not about playing the martyr and taking full responsibility. It is about acknowledging and accepting your role, even if you were not directly involved.

Here are some accepting attitudes and behavior examples you might say to yourself and other teammates.

> *I have played a part in creating this situation by not being willing to let my teammates help me with my projects.*
>
> *I promoted this situation by not telling the teammate when their performance was below standard.*
>
> *I have allowed this situation to occur by not openly expressing my concerns about the uneven workload distribution with the whole team.*

Forgive

Once you've acknowledged and accepted your part in this situation, you must forgive and let go of what has happened prior to this point in time.

This is not about letting yourself or your teammates off the hook. In fact, it's precisely the opposite. All teammates must own their part. But if you cannot forgive and let go of what has already happened, where will that unforgiving attitude take you and the team? You will go down to the wrong-minded, victim path.

You cannot change what has already happened. You can only change things from this point forward. That is why forgiveness is an essential step.

Forgiving others releases you from wanting to know "why" something happened and stops you from focusing on past behaviors. It frees you from the need to blame others for the problem, and it helps you focus on fixing the situation by agreeing on what needs to happen going forward.

> *The Right-Minded choice path's first three steps – acknowledge, accept, forgive – can be accomplished very quickly. Sometimes they may take just a few minutes.*

The more you practice the Right Choice thinking system, the more likely it is that you will be able to achieve these three steps quickly when difficult situations arise.

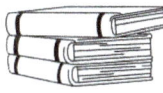 **To Learn More…**

"I forgive myself and others" is Lesson #4 in *7 Lessons Mindful Training Lessons: Improve Teammates' Ability to Work as One* with Right-Minded Thinking. In this RMT book, available at RightMindedTeamwork.com, you will find more instructions and justification for practicing forgiveness with yourself and your teammates.

Adjust

To acknowledge, accept, and forgive frees you to adjust your attitudes without self-judgment. You are now in the proper frame of mind to come up with viable alternative solutions.

Whereas the first three steps of the upper loop of the Right Choice Model can happen very quickly, adjusting takes longer to accomplish. Depending on the situation, adjusting could take a few hours or even several days.

It is in this step that you return to your Right Mind. You accept your moment of Reason, free your mind of unforgiving thoughts, and trust your Decision-Maker's intuition. You remind yourself:

I am here only to be truly helpful.

I am here to represent Reason, who sent me.

I do not have to worry about what to say or what to do because Reason, who sent me, will direct me.

You bring in Reason's gentle guidance towards oneness, and you restore your mind to the forgiving Unified Circle of Right-Minded Thinking. In this open, receptive mindset, you are able to receive viable alternative solutions as to how to adjust, respond, and heal your challenging situation.

Returning to our example, let's say that you have now experienced three separate instances where your teammate did not perform their job very well. You are now noticing a pattern of subpar work.

Listening to Reason and your Decision-Maker's intuition, you decide to approach the teammate in a private conversation. You also choose only to discuss the most recent incident, not the pattern, because you know that if you create a new Work Agreement to address the problem, they will most likely improve going forward.

You approach the poor-performing teammate in a Right-Minded way, as follows.

Set a positive stage.

> *Dan, may I talk with you about the XYZ project? I'm a little uneasy about discussing this with you because it's about you. I certainly don't want to offend.*
>
> *And this may be more about me and my standards. If it is, I will be willing to change.*
>
> *Anyway, I'm sure both of us want to be certain we're aligned on our team roles, responsibilities, and deliverables.*

Describe the situation in a factual, neutral way.

> *While working together on the XYZ project, you called Samantha and negotiated a new deadline before talking with me first.*

State what you want for yourself, NOT what you want the other person to do.

I want to have input in setting deadlines for projects I'm working on. How can we make that happen?

Listen. Explore solutions. Make Work Agreements.

I am glad we talked about this situation. To repeat back for both of us, we've agreed that if new deadlines are discussed in the future, we will make the decision together. We also decided that if either one of us thinks the other is not doing the right work right, we have permission to discuss and resolve it. Do I have that right?

There are infinite versions of such Right-Minded conversations. This example is just one scenario. But there is one fundamental principle to follow in every adjustment: If plan A doesn't work, go to plan B.

That means if the teammate breaks your new Work Agreement, you simply follow the Right Choice steps once more by acknowledging, accepting, forgiving, and then approaching the teammate to create and agree to plan B.

The key here is to always come up with new options, and not give up if your first try doesn't work the way you want. You may not solve things correctly the first time, but as long as you remain willing to try different solutions, you will find one that works.

Recover

Recovery is the direct result of your willingness to change your attitude and behavior about your teammate. With your honest discussion that led to a Work Agreement to solve the problem, you have both adjusted; now it is time to move forward by following your new Work Agreement.

When you and your teammate follow your Agreement, you create your own evidence that the Right Choice Model, Work Agreements, and Right-Minded Teamwork process work. Your success encourages you both to continue listening to Reason's reliable guidance.

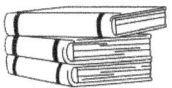 *To Learn More...*

Watch a *video* now!

For video instruction on applying the Right Choice Model steps and concepts, visit RightMindedTeamwork.com, and search for ***How to Apply the Right Choice Model***.

On the product page for the book, you will find a video titled, *"Right Choice Cards & Right Choice Behavior."*

Summarizing Right-Minded Choices

By acknowledging, accepting, forgiving, adjusting, and recovering, will you deal with difficult situations effectively?

Absolutely.

When you follow the Right Choice path through the upper loop of the Right Choice Model, you demonstrate that you have successfully unlearned those wrong-minded, Ego attitudes. Joining with Reason and your teammates, you actively live your Right Choice Work Agreements.

By consistently applying Right Choice and using Right-Minded attitudes and behaviors, you quickly move into a problem-resolving mode when stressful situations occur. Each time a difficult situation arises, you and your teammates cycle through the upper-loop Right Choice behaviors even faster.

The act of uniting is your declaration of interdependence. It is your moment of Reason and your return to the Unified Circle of Right-Minded Thinking. It is your statement of solidarity and belief that mindful truths are self-evident and that all minds are created equal.

It is your commitment to **do no harm** as you **work as one**.

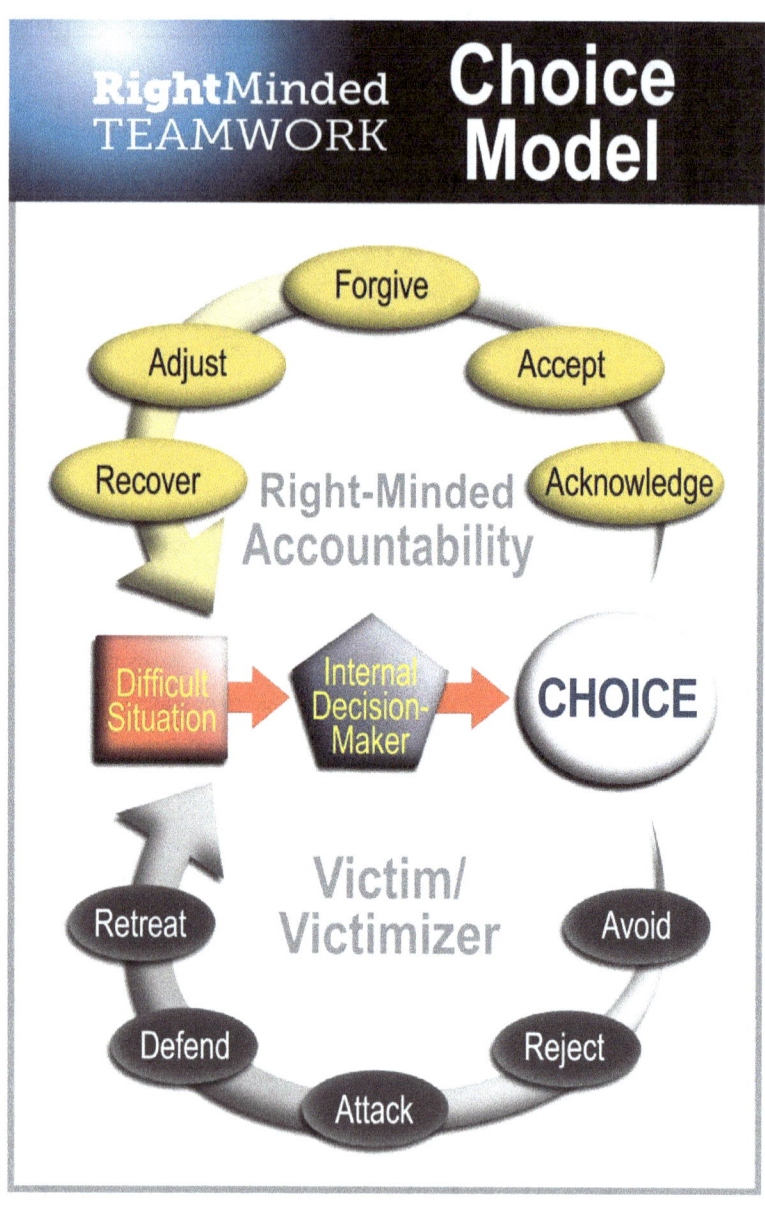

How to Present & Apply the Right Choice Model in Your Team

Now that you know how to apply the Right Choice Model personally, let's move into learning how to present and apply it to your team. Here, we'll expand upon one of the options mentioned earlier in the section entitled, *How Does a Team Use the Right Choice Model?*

In that section, we briefly discussed a difficult team situation where the team's primary customer was disappointed in the team's product or service quality. Now, let's learn more about how the team leader presented and applied the Right Choice Model in their team problem-solving meeting.

Presenting Right Choice

When you present the Right Choice concepts in a team-building workshop, your objective is to help your team embrace Right-Minded accountability while discussing the team's challenging issue - in this case, a dissatisfied customer.

Some teammates will not be as skilled as others at discussing these kinds of attitudes and behaviors. That's okay; they don't need to be at this moment. Expecting them to thoroughly learn the Model's concepts in the first presentation is not your aim.

Your only goal in your first presentation is to present the Model in such a way that all teammates declare,

> *Of course, we need to **approach our customer's disappointment in our service** in a Right-Minded, accountable way. Let's get started.*

It's best to stick with a short presentation. Four to five minutes will suffice.

As soon as all teammates are in the right frame of mind, stop presenting, and move everyone into a team discussion where all teammates discuss and agree on how to solve their problem.

In this conversation, teammates use "upper loop attitudes" while discussing the issue. The discussion eventually leads to creating Work Agreements that teammates believe will resolve their issues.

After the workshop, teammates follow their new Work Agreements, improving their teamwork and productivity. In time, because they have become more effective, your team has an even happier customer.

Applying Right Choice: A Real-World Example

I worked with an Accounts Payable team of 15 teammates, plus the team leader. The team supported six large operating divisions. Every teammate was assigned to one or two specific operating divisions.

One of the team's customers, an operating division leader, had recently informed the team leader that five out of the six key vendors they used for the last seven months were not paid on time.

This poor service was causing strained customer-vendor relationships for the operating division. The operations leader was very frustrated with the Accounts Payable department and wanted their vendors paid on time. They insisted the A/P department fix the problem now.

HOW TO APPLY THE RIGHT CHOICE MODEL · 101

The team leader decided the best way to address and resolve this situation was to conduct a problem-resolution session. He called an emergency meeting with all 15 A/P teammates. Everyone was asked to meet in the conference room in one hour.

To prepare, the leader printed the Right Choice Cards to give to each teammate at the meeting.

An hour later, everyone was in the meeting room. The leader said,

We have a difficult situation. All of us need to band together to resolve it. Let me explain.

The leader shared the details. The leader acknowledged the A/P department appeared to be paying the other five operating division's vendors on time. He went on to say,

Even though some of you are not directly involved with this situation, we are an interdependent team. We look out for and support one another.

After we resolve this situation, we may likely need to use our new process improvements in all A/P functions. We will see, but we need to discuss and agree on how we will resolve the current problem now.

Before we start brainstorming potential solutions, I want to take just a few minutes to make sure we're all in the right frame of mind.

Recently, I saw this. It's called the Right Choice Model. [The leader distributes the Right Choice Cards to all.] It's a simple way to describe right and wrong ways to address challenges like ours.

> *The model teaches that we only have two choices regarding how we respond to challenges like this one. We either embrace and demonstrate Right-Minded attitudes and accountable behaviors, or we can lower ourselves into wrong-minded, victim behaviors.*
>
> *Right Choice says, as you can see in the upper loop, we first need to acknowledge what has happened and accept our role in the situation. The third step is to forgive, or, if you prefer, stop blaming ourselves or others.*
>
> *I firmly believe we can resolve this problem if we accept responsibility and forgive ourselves for what has happened. When we do that, we will create the right frame of mind to complete the last two steps of adjusting and recovering from this situation.*
>
> *Our only other choice is to reject, attack, or defend, as you can see listed in the lower loop. If we go there, which is the wrong frame of mind, we will not resolve this problem. We are much better than that.*
>
> *We are, by being here together right now, acknowledging this situation. We are accepting and owning our individual and team roles in this situation. And for goodness's sake, let's forgive ourselves and others so that we can be in the right frame of mind to find the best solutions.*
>
> *Shall we all commit to demonstrating Right-Minded, upper-loop, accountable behaviors in today's meeting so we can successfully recover and regain our customer's trust?*

Everyone agreed. The leader continued,

> *Okay, great. What do we know about the situation, and what might be potential solutions?*

Teammates brainstormed for two hours and created new Work Agreements to streamline and speed up the payment process.

The next day, the leader and two A/P teammates presented their work process improvement ideas to the operations leader.

All agreed that the new methods should work. The operations leader contacted the five vendors and explained the new process. The vendors were appreciative and cautiously optimistic. They agreed to wait and see if the new method was effective.

Summary of the Right Choice Process Steps

In this story, you can easily see the basic formula for presenting the Right Choice Model in your team:

- Present the Right Choice Model using the context of the team's current difficult situation. Ask teammates to act in an accountable way while they discuss how to resolve their team problem.

- Conduct a problem-resolution discussion that leads to a deeper understanding and possible solutions.

- Create Work Agreements the team believes will correct the team's mistakes.

- Follow and live the Work Agreements to recover and achieve customer satisfaction.

In this situation, after learning about the difficult situation, the leader knew everyone on the team needed to band together to resolve it. The leader shared the dissatisfied customer's story with everyone, then used the Right Choice Model and Cards to create the right mindset for solving their problem. His presentation only lasted a few minutes.

Then he transitioned the conversation into team talk, a problem-resolution discussion to brainstorm solutions. The exchange resulted in Work Agreements that streamlined workflows and processes.

The team went back to the A/P's customer to share their solutions, and they looped in the vendor as well.

Following the team's implementation of their solutions, the vendor payments were never late again.

RightMinded TEAMWORK Choice Model

Right-Minded Accountability
- Forgive
- Accept
- Acknowledge
- Recover
- Adjust

Difficult Situation → Internal Decision-Maker → CHOICE

Victim/Victimizer
- Avoid
- Reject
- Attack
- Defend
- Retreat

Applications for the Right Choice Model

The Right-Minded Teamwork Choice Model and Work Agreement tools are perfect for those situations where logic and other fact-based processes don't work. Here are several instances where these concepts and tools lend themselves well.

Team Building – When a team is "storming," these tools will help you facilitate a positive recovery in team members' attitudes and behaviors.

Benefit: The team focuses more energy on accomplishing real team business versus complaining about other team members.

Leadership Development – Successful leaders are people who can, among other things, guide their direct reports to higher and higher levels of accountability, an inherent result of Right Choice and Work Agreements.

Benefit: The team addresses problems head-on versus whining and complaining about life's difficult work situations.

Safety – The Right Choice Model is a perfect companion for behavioral safety strategies and training programs because "choice" is the precursor to "safe" behavior.

Benefit: Add the final layer of understanding in safety training – a "thinking system."

Diversity – People who do not embrace diversity are making wrong-minded, victimizer choices.

Benefit: This Model will help you surface those disconnects and create Agreements for higher levels of collaboration.

Alliance Partnerships – Too often, partnerships break up or fail to meet expectations because of the business's attitudes and behaviors.

Benefit: This Model will help you surface such issues so that they are dealt with in an emotionally mature way. The energy previously being put towards dysfunctional behaviors can instead be transformed to accomplishing the alliance's work.

Change Management – Consultants and leaders can use this process in all their change initiatives.

Benefit: This Model will increase the likelihood of success by removing or transforming restraining forces.

Individual Effectiveness – We all feel and act like victims from time to time. The key is not getting stuck in a victim's headspace. To avoid getting stuck, we must identify those situations that drive us into the Right Choice Model's lower loop: wrong-mindedness.

Benefit: The Right Choice Model, when used as a personal assessment, helps you identify personal emotional triggers, which is the first step in effective change management.

Outsourcing – This Model will not stop outsourcing, but it will help ensure a smooth transition.

Benefit: By identifying those who are more apt to accept and embrace change (versus those who act and behave like they are entitled to special treatment), outsourcing is more likely to succeed.

Others – The possibilities for the Right Choice Model and Work Agreement process are genuinely endless. Literally anywhere you find people in conflict, this process will assist you in facilitating positive transformation.

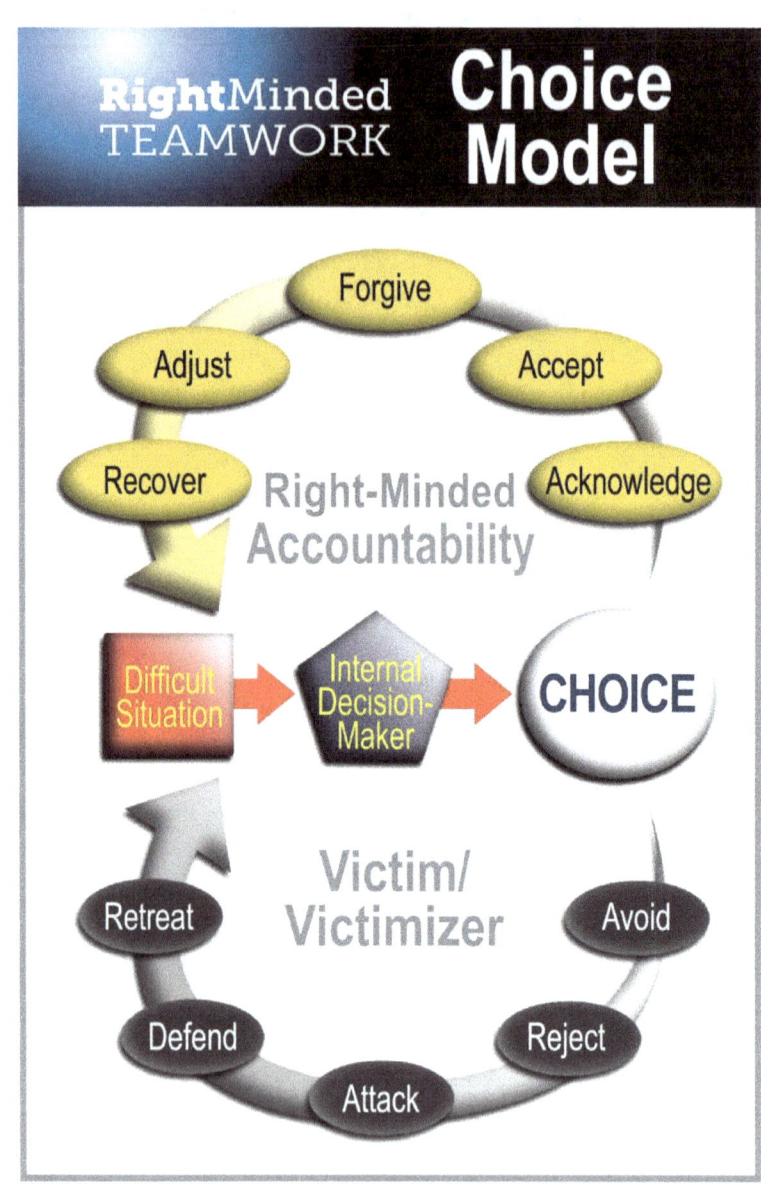

Everything Else About the Right Choice Model

Key Concepts

1. The **only freedom** you truly have is the freedom to choose.

2. Freedom is the **desire, willingness, and ability to change one's principles,** values, and behaviors in order to choose right over wrong-mindedness and accountability over victimization.

3. To claim this freedom, **you must train your mind**. This is about teaching yourself to think differently, to think in a more emotionally mature, more responsible, and more accountable, Right-Minded way.

4. **At every moment, you are making one of two choices**. Those choices are either accountability or victimization. It is impossible to choose neither, nor can you choose both. It is always one or the other.

5. Even though it is undesirable, the reality is that we all are continually moving back and forth between accountability and victimization. This doesn't make us bad people; we are simply confused and conflicted. For each of us, though, **our life goal is to experience more Right-Mindedness than wrong-mindedness.**

6. The **Right Choice Model is a "thought system,"** or mental model, that helps us recognize wrong-minded thoughts and shift them into Right-Minded choices and actions. It deals with cause, not effect. This is noticeably different from many other growth approaches, which deal with behaviors, rewards, and recognition.

   For example, team games do not deal with how a person thinks. They deal with play, which is not likely to change a person's thought system. Additionally, personality assessments can be useful, but if they do not advocate that anyone can change their personality, then it is just another mindless team-building approach.

7. **Thoughts, by their very nature, are creative; we produce what we perceive**. Our thoughts produce our behaviors, which we can see through our Decision Maker's choices.

8. Many of us operate in a state of insanity, thinking and acting the same way repeatedly and expecting different results. Think about this. You would not excuse insane behavior on your part by saying you could not help it. Why, then, would you condone insane thinking when you know you have the power to change your mind?

9. The Right Choice Model begins the process of restoring your **power of choice**. *That power* gives you (the Decision-Maker) back your freedom.

10. The experience of the **victim/victimizer furthers the de-evolution of the self.**

    The experience of the **accountable/responsible person furthers the evolution of the self.**

    When we are accountable and responsible, we are declaring that our behaviors do not imprison us, that we are a conscious Decision-Maker with a **New Mind** who makes the intentional choice to be accountable and responsible.

11. We determine our accountability or victimization within our relationships with others. Essentially, **all our relationships are classrooms**, or practice fields, for personal growth. If you see your relationships from Ego's perspective, you will turn your classrooms into battlegrounds. Or you can actively and consciously follow Reason, choosing to learn and practice responsible principles and values in all your relationships. The choice is yours: classrooms or battlegrounds?

12. All terms, like the ones in this Model, are potentially controversial. **Those who seek controversy will find it.** Those who seek clarification will find it as well. To understand this Model – this Right Choice thought system – you must be willing to overlook controversy.

13. Philosophical speculation and theoretical considerations are also controversial. They depend on belief and can, therefore, be accepted or rejected. A universal philosophy, theory, or model is impossible. Still, **striving for a universal experience**, like the one the Right Choice Model describes, is possible and, according to the Model, necessary for creating a functional and worthwhile life.

14. Understanding how the Right Choice Model works is only the first step in making a positive change in your life.

    The second step is to make different choices, ones aligned with your **New Mind**. Right Choice Work Agreements are powerful tools to help you on your way.

Principles & Values

Whether they are conscious or unconscious, **everyone functions based on principles and values**. They exist in teams, organizations, and you. They are continuously operating in your life. They guide your choices, whether or not you are aware of their influence.

1. **A principle is timeless, self-evident, and self-validating.** It is a universal pillar of truth.

   A value is something you hold dear. It is your interpretation of what you believe to be a principle. Values are what matters to you, what you'll stand for, or and what you'll speak up for. They are a cause you believe in.

2. Your **principles and values are like a film projector**. You're continually projecting what's in your mind and heart by putting your "spin" or interpretation onto all you're seeing, hearing, and experiencing. This is why some people can see or interpret the same situation entirely differently.

3. If your principles and values are mainly like those listed in the **Right-Minded Teamwork Attitudes & Behaviors** list found earlier in this book, you'll live a more peaceful and fulfilling life. However, if your attitudes are more like the ones on the wrong-minded list, your life will feel miserable and painful to you.

   For example, holding and nurturing the thought, **"It's a vengeful world out there,"** is an indicator you retain attacking thoughts in your mind. **Having projected your anger and fear onto the world,** you constantly see vengeance about to strike you.

Because you see yourself as being attacked, your own outward attacks are perceived and justified as self-defense. Your behavior reinforces your belief, and this **increasingly vicious cycle** continues until you are willing to change how you see the situation. If you do not change, thoughts of attack and counterattack will indefinitely continue to preoccupy your mind, making your life more and more miserable. **Peace of mind will be impossible.**

Are you ready to escape? You can. This battleground is not real. **You can escape the victimization mindset by merely choosing to change your mind**, training yourself intentionally to think in a new way (for specifics, refer back to the section of this book where we talked about the Constantly Complaining Teammate, called *Choosing Your Team's Right Attitudes & Behaviors*.)

4. Right-Minded **principles and values are quiet and secure in themselves;** wrong-minded beliefs and values are loud and insecure. Right-Mindedness uncovers the song of gratitude behind the screams of wrong-minded principles or values.

5. Right-Minded principles and **values can and should become habitual**. If they are not showing up regularly in your life, something has gone wrong.

6. Each time you act, you consciously or unconsciously align yourself with the principles and values you believe will bring you the most benefit or reward. In so doing, you engage either your **Old Mind** or your **New Mind**.

7. **Your Old Mind is your reactive, reptilian mind.** It promotes your instinctual needs and reactions, such as eating, sleeping, and physical safety. It also includes your beliefs and attachments that relate to your emotional safety. Old Mind directives include staying alive and staying safe. When the Old Mind is overtaxed, you get reactive and defensive.

8. **Your New Mind is that part of you that is proactive.** It moves you towards greater self-awareness and self-actualization. New Mind directives are to explore, build, and create. **New Mind believes there must be a better way.**

9. Key people in your life, such as your spouse or partner, parents, coworkers, etc., are **Primary Person Symbols (PPS).**

    When a PPS makes an undesirable change in their behavior towards you, it activates any unresolved issues or past experiences you have had with all the PPS givers in your life.

    Your triggered response to the change in their behavior stems mainly from your Old Mind.

10. When you are proactively attempting to embrace New Mind principles and values, clear Work Agreements form a mutually agreed-upon basis for changing behaviors.

    Creating a Work Agreement to solve a challenging interpersonal problem is a true New Mind activity. Your Old Mind would never think of doing such a thing.

11. **The more time you spend in the New Mind**, the less comfortable you will be spending time in your Old Mind. However, if you currently spend most of your time in your Old Mind, attempting to move to the New Mind will seem like a painful experience.

    Therefore, you must make a conscious and intentional choice to make the change from Old Mind to New Mind, despite the pain. In this case, **it is preferable to make small and secure steps towards your New Mind** rather than trying to do it all at once.

12. When you apply your mind with focused concentration, **it will produce self-fulfilling prophecies**. What you produce is always from either the Old Mind or New Mind, depending on which you are focused.

Principles and values are with us every moment of every single day. As the story below illustrates, it is up to us to focus on the Right-Minded ones.

> *Two men were walking down a crowded sidewalk in a downtown business area. Suddenly one exclaimed, "Listen to the lovely sound of that cricket!"*
>
> *The other man could not hear it. He asked his companion how he could detect the sound of the cricket amidst the din of people and traffic. The first man knew he could hear it because, as a zoologist, he had trained himself to listen for the sounds of nature.*
>
> *Instead of explaining, he took a coin from his pocket and dropped it on the sidewalk. Immediately, a dozen people spun around to look at them. "We hear what we listen for," said the zoologist.*

You, too, will see and hear what your principles and values tell you.

Change Happens

Change not only happens, but it's happening at an increased rate.

It is easy to see how this statement is true when you look at the history of humankind from a much broader perspective. Humans have been on this planet for 50,000 years. To illustrate, imagine you compress that span of 50,000 years into 50 years.

Relatively speaking…
- It was only ten years ago that the last of your neighbors moved out of their caves.
- Two years ago, Jesus Christ was born.
- Eighteen months ago, mass communication began, thanks to the invention of the printing press.
- Ten days ago, Edison brought us the use of electricity.
- Yesterday, the first airplane flew.
- Last night, the radio was invented.
- This morning, the TV was created.

As you can see, most of these changes have been in the last 18 months of your 50 years.

That is an incredible rate of change! And technology just keeps getting faster.

Change Is Inevitable; Resisting It Changes Nothing

Changes are neither positive nor negative.

You *choose* to experience them as positive, negative, or neutral.

The way you react to situations and changes either perpetuates problems or helps to resolve them. All changes are opportunities for learning how to make better choices.

There are two types of changes that tend to trigger inappropriate emotional behaviors:

1. Reality does not live up to your expectations
   (your current reality $\neq$ your future hope).

   - You were not given that new and exciting job
   - After careful examination, you cannot afford that new car you want
   - Due to weather conditions, your best friend's plane was canceled

2. You perceive offensive and inappropriate behavior from another person.

   - Someone tells an off-color joke
   - You are accused of something you did not do
   - Someone attacks or belittles your work performance
   - You are treated as "less than" by others in authority who believe they are "better than"

What other kinds of situations or changes can you think of that trigger you into victimization?

The Decision-Maker

Your choice on how you react to change comes down to your "Decision-Maker," a term created for this Model to help you identify **the aspect of "you" that is choosing**. Your Decision-Maker can also be thought of as your inner voice or your intuition. It is functioning all the time, even while you are asleep. You are either conscious or unconscious of your Decision-Maker.

- Your Decision-Maker is that part of you that **holds the power to choose.** It is like a valve that regulates the flow of all your choices. It cannot be neutral; it is always open to either Right or wrong-mindedness.

- The **Decision-Maker is what learns**, and the thinking system it supports is either that of the Old (wrong) Mind or the New (Right) Mind. All learning moves you towards Right or wrong-mindedness.

- **Is perception reality or fact? Neither**. It's a choice as to what you want to see, a projection of what your Decision-Maker is holding front and center (which will always be either accountable or victimized principles).

- In extreme situations, your Decision-Maker *should choose* **FLIGHT**.

  Extreme conditions include verbal, emotional, psychological, or physical abuse and physical or life-threatening danger. Afterward, when things have calmed down and you become safe, you can ask yourself, "What did I do to set up or contribute to getting myself into this situation, and what can I do differently the next time something like this happens?"

- For the **person who is stuck in the wrong-minded lower loop of the Right Choice Model**, their whole existence feels like one of victimization. It seems to them that being a victim and being a victimizer are the only two choices available. It's as though they have shut themselves off from their other real choice. They are so caught up in either being a victim or victimizer that they **don't even see there's another way of looking at the situation.**

- Lack of conscious awareness of your Decision-Maker increases the likelihood of making more victimized choices. Heightened awareness of the Decision-Maker (the mindful ability to observe yourself making choices) **increases the likelihood and frequency of choosing accountable behaviors.**

Choosing Wrong-Mindedness

The choice for wrong-mindedness is often an unconscious, **Egocentric reaction – an Old Mind response.**

When you choose wrong-mindedness, your attention automatically attaches itself to the situation. You continue to think about it, and if you stop long enough to watch yourself, you'll discover you are obsessing over it.

In some instances, your obsession will fill you with the desire to avoid, deny, or run away. Sometimes, it will even paralyze you, keeping you stuck where you are. In other instances, the situation may mobilize you into action. To prove you are right, you either move to attack or defend, neither of which effectively solves the problem or improves the situation.

Wrong-Mindedness: Fight, Flight, or Freeze

- **Fighting** is when you aggressively or passive-aggressively stand your ground and argue or defend your position regarding the situation or change.

- **Flight** is when you physically, emotionally, or mentally withdraw or disengage.

- **Freezing** is when you become immobilized physically, emotionally, or mentally regarding the situation or change.

- Fight, flight, and freeze are easier than going with the **flow** because they don't require any change on your part.

- When you choose to fight, flee, or freeze, it means you do not feel safe enough to make a change in yourself. As long as you tell yourself things are unsafe and continue to perceive a lack of safety, you will remain in the wrong-mindedness loop.

- Flow is, for the most part, a synonym for Right-Mindedness. Going with the flow (by embracing the subsequent behaviors of forgiving, learning, and recovering) requires you to change. Going with the flow may feel harder at first, but it gets easier and easier the more you choose to lead with your Right Mind.

Fight Language

I must protect myself!

You [or they or it] are my problem!

I feel like a scapegoat, and it's unfair.

I'm the victim here, and I feel angry and resentful!

This situation just proves I was right and that they don't like me, want me, appreciate me, respect me, include me, etc.

I'm going to others to argue my position regarding why I'm right, and they're wrong.

I'm attempting to manipulate the situation to my advantage by planting information or withholding information; this will get me into power struggles with others, but I don't care because I'm right about this one!

Flight Language

My buttons are pushed, and I'm not responsible for the way I'm behaving right now; it's their fault.

I'm not performing at my best because of this situation, and it's not my fault.

I feel helpless – hopeless.

I'm fed up with this _____ (situation, company, team, relationship, etc.).

I've had enough. I'm leaving!

Freeze Language

I'm constantly thinking about how I've been wronged. I can't seem to get it out of my mind.

I'm not pleasant to be around, even with my best friends.

I'm worried and anxious.

Wrong-Mindedness: Attack, Avoid, Defend

Allowing attack, avoid, or defend attitudes to enter your mind means you have not accepted forgiveness and learning as wholly desirable within the situation.

Attacking is when:

- You use an adversarial communication style – toxic body language, caustic tone of voice, and poor word choice.

- You quickly exclude contrary opinions in discussions.

- You consider only one or two alternatives in problem-solving or conflict resolution.

- You demonstrate resistance to everything except your personal opinion or solution.

- You sincerely believe you are right and that others ought to listen to you.

- You listen only to defend or respond.

- You use inappropriate words that trigger dysfunctional responses in others.

- You misrepresent others' statements by either lying or putting your spin on another's statements to change what they said completely.

- You flat-out blame others.

Avoiding is when:

- You exit situations quickly when interactions get awkward and tense.

- You avoid or hide from difficult situations. Contemporary forms of hiding include staying confused or saying that you're "too busy" with all the work you have on your plate.

Defending is when:

- You get into an elaborate intellectual rationalization explaining why you're right and others are wrong.

- You continue to justify why you did what you did, so the situation is not your fault – it's someone else's fault.

- You bring forward all the past wrongs that have happened to you and others (when people get historical, they get hysterical).

Wrong-Mindedness: Costs & Benefits

Every behavior generates some form of benefit or cost. Benefits and rewards validate principles and strengthen values while costs and consequences challenge values and call for change.

Before we actively change a principle or value, the benefit and reward for changing must outweigh the cost and consequence of not changing.

In wrong-mindedness, victims believe "it's not my fault;" victimizers think it's your fault. Neither attitude will change anything. However, those attitudes will ensure the victim remains a victim and the victimizer remains a victimizer.

Wrong-minded costs include:

- Unresolved problems are caused by people who are too busy attacking, avoiding, defending, or freezing instead of solving issues

- Loss of trust

- Increased tension and stress

- Decreased productivity

- Mistakes are typically repeated, which has a ripple effect of creating more errors in jobs and relationships

- The situation stays the same, or attempts to change are sabotaged

- Resistance increases

- Negative reinforcement is increased, which creates a sense of helplessness and hopelessness

- New adversarial relationships and interactions are created

- Increased stress puts strain on the physical body, which causes negative changes in the cardiovascular system, immune system, and emotional center of the brain

- Emotional and psychological pain increase

- Fear increases; people don't feel safe

Wrong-minded "benefits" include:

- For the victimizer, a strong sense of "winning" the battle, which reinforces the belief that attack and blame are beneficial

- A temporary feeling of success because "my position was accepted; I was right all along!" (usually doesn't last)

- An elaborate interpersonal defense system

- Continued attacks stemming from a feeling of "I'm right, but nobody sees it, so I'm going to keep doing it"

Wrong-Minded (Old Mind) Principles & Values

When you hold onto wrong-minded or Old Mind principles and values, you are projecting what you don't want onto others. You are actively trying to get rid of your fears because it's so painful to hold onto them.

The only possible result of these principles and values is to create a battleground in your life.

Battlegrounds are:

- Confusion, chaos, and complexity

- Total or shared victimization

- Total or shared victimizer behavior

- Mindless, habit-centered behavior

- Attitudes of "it's hell on earth," "it's a dog-eat-dog world out there," "it's kill or be killed," or "win or lose."

- The belief that everyone's an adversary – "I can't trust anyone!"

- Non-productive and ineffective individuals or teams

- Unhealthy, immature, destructive, attack-and-defend interpersonal "dances"

- The belief that people are basically bad at their core; you've got to protect yourself

- A belief that it's not okay to make mistakes; others will use them against you

- A belief that you can't be seen or thought of as vulnerable

- A belief that you've got to fight for everything you get because you're a _____

- A belief that "they caused my pain" and that "they need to stop" before I can feel better

- Feelings of insecurity and a lack of safety

- A belief that "they're out to get me," so I must protect myself

Results of Battleground Thinking & Behaving:

- The situation stays the same or gets worse. The change doesn't produce the desired outcome; you still feel the pain of the situation.

- No agreements or solutions for making things better are created.

- A self-perpetuating attack-and-defend "dance" starts between all those involved; soon, everyone feels they've been victimized.

Choosing Right-Mindedness

When you're in your Right Mind, your focus is on Reason's principles and your team Work Agreements.

You do not succumb to the enticing, almost intoxicating lure of attack, avoid, and defend. Instead, you opt to forgive, learn, and recover from difficult situations.

Your principles determine how you respond to the situation, not the other way around. You accept the realization that you have a kingdom to rule, so you consistently choose the path of Right Choice and Right-Mindedness, even in the direst of situations.

Right-Minded Steps to Take When a Difficult Situation Happens

1. Acknowledge and look at the situation. Don't avoid or deny it.

2. Own that the situation affects you: it bothers, frustrates, or worries you. "Call it out" to others involved in a non-attacking, non-blaming way.

   Recognizing the impact of the situation is like shooting up a flare in the night sky so all involved can see the issue. You could start the conversation by saying something like, "I would like to learn a new way of interacting with you regarding _____ (i.e., keeping commitments, communication style, respect for others). Would you please talk with me about this?"

3. Own your part in the situation. Instead of blaming others or denying your role, ask yourself how you created, promoted, or allowed this situation or change to occur. Also, own that you are creating your emotions. Owning your part brings your power back to you.

Getting into a Right-Minded Flow

- The law of change states that relationships never stay the same; people are always either moving closer together or farther apart.

- Flow is about continuing the process of a group or team moving closer together, even while situations and changes challenge interpersonal relationships.

- Flow is moving towards the situation or change rather than away from it.

- Flow is the opposite of a "knee-jerk" reaction. Flow is taking a deep breath and taking time to think before you react. It is seeking a moment of Reason.

- Flow can also feel a lot like surrender because it's about riding the wave of change, not fighting or avoiding it. Surrender, in this context, does not mean giving up. It is about letting go of what's not working, about making a sacrifice of the right kind.

When you are in flow, you:

- Believe you are responsible for what you see in the situations and changes around you.

- Believe there must be a better way.

- Own that you don't care for another's behavior, but, knowing you're in charge of your reaction, choose not to be pulled into the battleground. Instead, you shift your perception, and now you see a learning opportunity in your classroom.

- Realize and embrace the fact that the way you were approaching or reacting was not working. Be sincerely willing to change yourself to make this situation or change better for yourself and others.

Right-Mindedness: Forgive, Learn, & Recover

Forgiving means:

- You don't hold it against yourself when you find you've been holding onto past grievances.

- In the present moment, you have released the past with the goal of recovering in the future.

- You are ready – intellectually and emotionally – to create Work Agreements to move your working relationships to a new level of maturity.

- You recognize the change in yourself based on your interactions with others involved. They sense you have overlooked, forgiven, and released the situation, and they become more agreeable to work out new solutions with you.

Learning means:

- You and the others involved let go of the old way and make space to devise a new way of dealing with the situation or managing the change.

- All involved have dialogued and agreed to follow a new, win-win solution: your Work or Action Agreement.

Recovering means:

- You and others have not wasted time blaming or rationalizing why the old way didn't work. Instead, you have spent your time and energy learning a new way and then implementing your new, agreed-upon solution.

- Understanding that sometimes your recovery is immediate, but most of the time, results may take a while.

  Important: Most first-time recovery solutions don't work as perfectly as you wish. Therefore, all involved must be willing to find yet another solution if the first solution doesn't work.

When you forgive, learn, and recover, you:

- Use an ally-building communication style.

- Offer new alternatives and solutions.

- Demonstrate willingness and active support for trying new solutions.

- Listen to understand others' alternatives, practicing empathic listening.

- Seek answers from others outside the group.

- Stay in relationships long enough to find a win-win solution or Work Agreement.

- Take collective or individual ownership of mistakes and successes.

- Forgive honest mistakes. Believe in recovery, and spend energy finding new options. Look for the possibilities in proposed solutions instead of focusing on all the reasons why something will not work.

Right-Mindedness: Rewards & Consequences

Those who choose Right-Mindedness participate in making their situations better and managing the change toward the desired outcome.

Just as with wrong-mindedness, there are costs, or consequences to choosing Right-Mindedness. However, the rewards of Right-Mindedness far outweigh the costs.

Consequences of Right-Mindedness:

- It takes more time to work things out than it does to attack, avoid, or defend.

- It's also painful at times to go through the process of making Agreements with others. There is usually emotional pain in letting go of a firmly-held position.

- People have to become more vulnerable by acknowledging their imperfections. They have to let go of fear, pain, stress, lack of safety, and victimization.

Rewards of Right-Mindedness:

- Problems are resolved. Mistakes are forgiven and forgotten.

- When conflicts arise, people move towards them and create new Agreements.

- New learning takes place.

- People are happier. There is more acknowledgment and appreciation.

- There seems to be enough abundance for everyone.

- New solutions are found. Obstacles are removed.

- Healthy, mature, constructive inquiry and recovery "dances" are created.

- People give others the benefit of the doubt.

- More productive, effective, and conscious individuals and teams are created.

Right-Minded (New Mind) Principles & Values

Benefits and rewards validate principles and strengthen values.

When you hold onto Right-Minded principles and values, you are actively trying to expand these values in yourself and share them with others. This is how you create a Right-Minded classroom at work and in your life.

Classrooms are:

- A place where people take total or shared accountability and/or responsibility

- A place where people are happier and don't take things so seriously

- Where people get acknowledged and appreciated and receive positive reinforcement

- Where people are forgiven for making honest mistakes

- Where people pull together and find faster, cheaper, better ways of getting quality work done

- Full of abundance mentality, the belief that there is always more than enough

- A place where it is fun to find new solutions

- Where it's okay to realize that our actions are the obstacle

- Where it's accepted that we are not our mistakes

- A place where people feel confident that all relationship problems can be resolved

- A peaceful and fun place

- Where people believe others are basically good people

- Where people realize their interpretations and reactions to others' behaviors are what's causing their pain

- A place where people realize life is a journey, not an end; a process, not a goal

Results of Classroom Thinking & Behaving:

- The situation improves. The change produces the desired result. Work Agreements and other solutions make the situation better.

- A new, self-perpetuating team culture of acknowledgment and support, forgiveness and recovery, is established among all involved.

The End.
Your New Beginning.

When all 5 Elements of Right-Minded Teamwork's core framework are fully released into your team's operating system, **especially your Right Choice Work Agreements**, you have established the proper conditions for your new beginning towards successfully achieving Right-Minded Teamwork.

Imagine This Future State

You are now thinking and behaving in a Right-Minded way. You are self-aware and focused on achieving your **team's business** and **psychological goals**. You consistently strive for **100% customer satisfaction**, and you always choose to **do no harm** while **working as one.**

To guide your steps, you have purposeful team **Work Agreements** describing your team's thought system – your Right Choices. You get work done by leveraging your Team Operating System, identifying the critical-few, focusing on solutions, and making true improvements.

As Right-Minded Teammates, you willingly follow Reason, behaving mindfully and positively navigating difficult team situations. You have risen far above Ego's battleground to joyfully engage with one another in your work classroom, learning and growing every day. Happily, you find yourselves living more and more often in the **Unified Circle of Right-Minded Teamwork Thinking.**

Your New Beginning

Now that you understand each of RMT's 5 Elements and how they will benefit your team, you are ready to implement RMT in your team. Remember, even though there is no right way to implement RMT, the three-workshop Implementation Plan presented earlier in these pages will always work.

So, gather your teammates, and conduct your first workshop. Live your new Right Choices and team Work Agreements for a month or two, then conduct the second workshop. Trust the process. Keep moving forward.

When you finish the third teammate development workshop, your team will begin following your customized 90-Day team operating plan. Every quarter, you will get to measure your progress and success. Each time, you will reinforce the value of RMT in your team.

Don't Forget!

As you begin your journey to Right-Minded Teamwork, don't forget: good teamwork does not just happen on its own. It must be cultivated, tended, and encouraged.

You need guidance from proven, real-world methods, such as Right-Minded Teamwork, to bring your team together. Moreover, you and your teammates must sincerely want to receive and follow this guidance, or the powerful teachings will be meaningless. Good teamwork must be a collaborative venture of commitment and growth.

If you want better teamwork, Right-Minded Teamwork can show you how to get there and what to do, but only with your help. Together with your teammates, you must believe that you have what it takes. With that conviction and Reason's guidance, you will collectively create and sustain Right-Minded Teamwork.

Now, go and create Right-Minded Teamwork for yourself and your team, and know that *you are making the world better for everyone, everywhere, forever.*

About the Author

The idea of "developing people and teams that work" began as a company statement for organizational consulting firm Lord & Hogan LLC, founded in 1990. Leveraging his personable but results-oriented consulting style, founder **Dan Hogan** devoted his career to transforming dysfunctional work relationships into positive, supportive bonds.

But over the course of his 40-year career, something shifted.

Through his work as an organizational development coach, performance consultant, and Certified Master Facilitator, the mission of Lord & Hogan also became Dan's own.

Better Work Relationships = Stronger, More Productive Teams

As a consultant and facilitator, Dan advocated for the individuals and managed teams he served. He emphasized the equal importance of strong team member relationships and solid business systems and processes to overall business success. His efforts spoke for themselves as his clients began to notice results.

With Dan's guidance, teams were more productive almost overnight. There were fewer day-to-day interpersonal issues. Project management efforts were finally back on track. Teams were achieving their goals.

After being stuck for so long, these teams were moving forward… smoothly. As one client said, "Dan has the unique ability to hear the confusion and bring clarity. He has helped me, our team, and our organization to move to the next level."

The Right-Minded Teamwork Model: A Legacy

Not only did Dan's efforts deliver consistent, powerful results (gaining him many long-term clients over the years) at a higher level, but his work also positively impacted the practice of behavioral change management.

Over the course of his career, Dan refined his ideas along with the help of his clients and the teams he served. Eventually, he created his own proprietary tools, processes, and strategies. Of all his models and creations, Dan's most significant accomplishment has been the development of his Right-Minded Teamwork model, which perfectly assembles all his tools and processes into a single, streamlined approach.

At its core, Right-Minded Teamwork (RMT) is a continuous improvement loop for small and large groups; it has been proven to work with teams of all sizes. No matter what team challenges or interpersonal issues are happening, RMT has the power to correct them.

By first bringing the team together under a unified set of goals, and then providing tools for teams to explore, understand, and work through their underlying concerns, Right-Minded Teamwork provides teams with the opportunity to address unproductive behaviors in a safe, non-condemning way. Focusing on acceptance, forgiveness, and self-adjustment among teammates, Right-Minded Teamwork directly addresses and resolves the root cause of even the most difficult teamwork situations.

After directly serving over 500 teams in seven countries and creating lasting tools and resources that will go on to support countless additional teams, leaders, and facilitators on every continent, Dan Hogan has left a legacy to be proud of. No longer an active facilitator, Dan has transformed his ideas and contributions into powerful, effective, team-building tools available online, providing team facilitators and team leaders around the globe access to Right-Minded Teamwork.

Books by Dan Hogan

Reason, Ego & the Right-Minded Teamwork Myth: *The Philosophy and Process for Creating a Right-Minded Team That Works Together as One*

This book explores two foundational concepts: the Right-Minded Teamwork Myth, a short tale that presents RMT's underlying teamwork philosophy, and the Right-Minded Teamwork team-building process, a step-by-step approach to implementing RMT in any team.

Right-Minded Teamwork in Any Team: *The Ultimate Team-Building Method to Create a Team That Works as One*

Right-Minded Teamwork is built on a framework of 5 Elements, explored in this book. These two goals and three methods are implemented into your team through three team-building workshops conducted over a six-to-12-month period. Once your team completes its third workshop, you move into a 90-day, continuous improvement operating plan that allows your team to achieve their goals, do no harm, and work together as one.

How to Facilitate Team Work Agreements: *A Practical, 10-Step Process for Building a Right-Minded Team That Works as One*

Team Work Agreements are collective pledges made by your team to transform non-productive or dysfunctional actions into positive and constructive work behavior. Though this book is written primarily for team facilitators, team leaders, and teammates may also follow these steps to create powerful, effective Work Agreements to solve and prevent interpersonal and process problems.

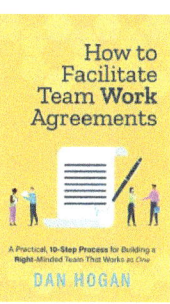

How to Apply the Right Choice Model: *Create a Right-Minded Team That Works as One*

The concept of Right Choice states every person has free will. Free will means you are 100% responsible for how you respond to every situation, circumstance, and event. When difficult team problems occur, you either act as an ally or an adversary. When you choose to be an ally, you demonstrate positive, accountable behavior. When you are an adversary, you behave as either a victim or a victimizer. This book and model will guide you through creating a team of productive, supportive, Right-Minded teammate allies.

7 Mindfulness Training Lessons: *Improve Teammates' Ability to Work as One with Right-Minded Thinking*

If you want your team to work together as one, you want them to think as one, too. These 7 Mindfulness Training Lessons will help you achieve a positive team mindset by guiding teammates to raise their awareness of thoughts, choices, and behaviors. Teammates may also use these lessons to create the team's Right-Minded thought system. The 7 Lessons can be summed up in one sentence, emphasizing three words: Right-Minded Teammates **accept**, **forgive**, and **adjust** their thinking and work behavior. When teammates follow these lessons, they **do no harm** while **working together as one.**

Right-Minded Teamwork: *9 Right Choices for Building a Team That Works as One*

This quick read is an excellent Right-Minded Teamwork primer and a terrific way to introduce RMT to teammates. These nine teamwork choices are universal, self-evident, and self-validating. You want them in your team. In this book, each of the 9 Right Choices is defined, and exercises are provided for applying each choice.

Design a Right-Minded, Team-Building Workshop:
12 Steps to Create a Team That Works as One

This book includes complete instructions on how to design a practical, real-world, team-building workshop that teammates actually want to attend. Unlike many team activities labeled "team building" that are really more "team bonding," true team-building workshops are intentionally designed to solve a team's real-world problems. Written primarily for team facilitators, team leaders, and teammates may also follow these 12 steps to design an effective, transformative team workshop.

Achieve Your Organization's Strategic Plan: *Create a Right-Minded Team Management System to Ensure All Teams Work as One*

When a single team within an organization works together as one, they are effective and productive. When an enterprise works with the same level of synergy, it is exponentially more powerful. A Team Management System like the Right-Minded Teamwork TMS model taught in this book lays the groundwork for your organization to get every team on the same page. By following RMT's four-part rollout plan, you can create and deploy your own Team Management System, align teammate attitudes, and work behavior with company values, and bring your entire organization together to work as one and achieve your strategic plan.

Glossary of Right-Minded Teamwork Terms & Resources

100% Customer Satisfaction

Creating 100% customer satisfaction is a primary goal of Right-Minded Teamwork. Your team is responsible for providing quality products and services to customers; for your team and enterprise to succeed, your customers deserve to be 100% satisfied.

With a strong customer satisfaction plan, as described in *Right-Minded Teamwork in Any Team*, your teammates will strive to achieve customer satisfaction while consistently achieving other business goals.

7 Mindfulness Training Lessons

Achieving Right-Minded Teamwork involves adopting an attitude of mindfulness. The *7 Mindfulness Training Lessons* teach you to think in a Right-Minded way, ensuring you **do no harm** as you **work as one** with your teammates.

These powerful lessons are summed up in one sentence, with emphasis on three words:

Right-Minded Teammates **accept**, **forgive**, *and* **adjust** *their thinking and work behavior.*

In every circumstance, especially during difficult team situations, Right-Minded Teammates practice mindfulness to move them from defensiveness and blame into a Right-Minded, allied way of thinking and behaving.

Inspired by *A Course in Miracles* and our Right Choice Model, the *7 Mindfulness Training Lessons* is a teaching tool designed to help those willing to apply them to ensure they return to the Unified Circle of Right-Minded Thinking.

Go to RightMindedTeamwork.com or visit your favorite book retailer to pick up your copy of *7 **Mindfulness Training Lessons***: *Improve Teammates' Ability to Work as One with Right-Minded Thinking.*

10 Characteristics of Right-Minded Teammates

Right-Minded Teammates have many different surface traits and personalities. They are not all alike. They have numerous backgrounds, vastly different experiences, and a wide range of skills.

Nevertheless, it is understood that the Right-Minded Teammate, in their own particular behavioral style, happily live these characteristics because they align the teammate's authentic *self* with their team's version of the RMT motto: *do no harm, work as one*, and *none of us is as smart as all of us.*

You will find a complete description of these characteristics in RMT's book: ***Right-Minded Teamwork in Any Team:*** *The Ultimate Team Building Method to Create a Team That Works as One.*

1. Trust	2. Honesty	3. Tolerance
4. Gentleness	5. Joy	6. Defenselessness
7. Generosity	8. Patience	9. Open-Mindedness
	10. Faithfulness	

12 Steps Workshop Design Process

Design a Right-Minded, Team-Building Workshop:*12 Steps to Create a Team That Works as One.* This book will teach you how to design a practical, real-world team-building workshop.

The 12 steps are grouped into three phases: Contract, Commence, and Carry on. Written primarily for team facilitators, team leaders, and teammates can easily follow the steps to design a successful team-building workshop. Because this method engages teammates in designing the agenda, it virtually guarantees that teammates *cannot wait* to attend the workshop. They *know* that they will get real work done in a safe, "no harm" environment when they meet.

A Course in Miracles

Oneness*.* Forgiveness is the key to happiness, inner peace, undifferentiated unity, and ultimately – *Oneness.* "A Course In Miracles (ACIM) is a unique spiritual self-study program designed to awaken us to the truth of our *Oneness* with God and Love," as posted on ACIM.org and ACIM.org/ACIM/en. See the Foundation for A Course in Miracles at FACIM.org, where Ken Wapnick, the founder, created this beautiful definition.

A Course in Miracles is a psychological approach to spirituality where forgiveness is the central theme, and inner peace is the result.

ACIM and other moral and spiritual philosophies that advocate and help people everywhere **work together as One** has inspired Right-Minded Teamwork. We used Ken's definition as a guide to create the Right-Minded Teamwork definition.

Right-Minded Teamwork is a business-oriented, psychological approach to team building where acceptance, forgiveness, and adjustments are teammate characteristics, and 100% customer satisfaction is the team's result.

All Right-Minded Teamwork methods, processes, and tools seamlessly work together to help you create and sustain a *Team That Works Together as* **One**.

Accept, Forgive, Adjust

These three terms are at the core of Right-Minded Teammate Attitudes & Behaviors. These verbs are also central to the *7 Mindfulness Training Lessons*, which are summed up in the sentence, *Right-Minded Teammates* **accept**, **forgive**, *and* **adjust** *their thinking and work behavior.*

Furthermore, these three concepts are included in the definition of Right-Minded Teamwork:

Right-Minded Teamwork is a business-oriented, psychological approach to team building where **acceptance**, **forgiveness**, *and* **adjustment** *are teammate characteristics, and 100% customer satisfaction is the team's result.*

Lastly, these terms are also incorporated as three of the five steps in the *Right Choice Model*, which describes accountable and responsible Right-Minded Teamwork behavior.

Ally or Adversary Teammate

Right-Minded Teamwork asserts that as teammates, you either work together as allies or pull apart, viewing each other as adversaries.

Allies work towards achieving team goals. Adversaries work towards individual elevation, which separates and divides the team.

To determine whether you are in an ally or adversary mindset, ask yourself, *Do I want to be right, or do I want our team to be successful?* Allies want to be part of a successful team. Adversaries want to be right, no matter the cost.

As an adversary, Ego persuades you to compete with your teammates. As an ally, Reason says the opposite. Reason gently reminds you that separateness prevents true success. There cannot be Oneness or collaboration where there is competition.

As the Decision-Maker, you choose to follow either Reason or Ego. You either collaborate or compete. You are an ally or adversary. There is no middle ground.

If you choose to follow Reason and become an ally, you embrace and live your team's Work Agreements. If you decide to follow Ego, you become an adversary, creating a battleground inside yourself and your team.

To transform competitive adversaries into collaborative allies, start by following the *Right Choice Model*, creating team *Work Agreements*, and applying the *7 Mindfulness Training Lessons*.

Avoidance Behavior

Even though the term "avoidance behavior" is not often mentioned in the Right-Minded Teamwork model or books, avoidance behavior is easy to detect in teammates and RMT processes. If you notice it occurring, from an RMT perspective, you can consider it wrong-minded, adversarial behavior.

Identifying avoidance behaviors and attitudes and understanding the harm they cause is the first step in moving from a wrong-minded place into Right-Mindedness. The *7 Mindfulness Training Lessons* and the *Right Choice Model* are excellent tools for teaching yourself and your team how to act and behave in a Right-Minded, accountable way.

For example, if you look carefully at the *Right Choice Model's* lower loop, you will notice that the victim or victimizer first avoids the situation when a difficult situation occurs.

When Right-Minded Teammates ask themselves the *Right Choice Model* question, *How did I **create**, **promote**, or **allow** this difficult situation to happen?* they often realize they have unconsciously demonstrated avoidance behavior. Then, noticing their mistake, they simply choose to **accept**, **forgive**, and **adjust** their approach and return to living in accordance with their team *Work Agreements*.

Battleground:
Where People Are Punished for Mistakes

The battleground represents wrong-minded thinking. It is a mental attitude or thought system that defends and encourages adversarial behaviors such as blame and attack.

Think of the battleground as a psychological symbol for those moments when you realize you are listening to Ego, not Reason (like when you notice avoidance behavior). You recognize that you are having an Ego attack for whatever reason and have made a wrong-minded choice. When you are in the battleground, you "punish" others for their mistakes, either by victimizing others or becoming a victim yourself.

On the other hand, when you are in your Right Mind, you see your team as a lovely and safe classroom, the opposite of the battleground. You do not punish others. You choose, instead, to rise above the conflict.

The purpose of recognizing the battlegrounds in your mind is to own the pain that you are causing yourself which helps you recognize that you consciously want to leave it, overlook it, rise above it, and to transport your mind into the classroom where you return to the forgiving Unified Circle of Right-Minded Thinking with your teammates.

Right-Minded Teammates working in safe and supportive classrooms do not fight, blame, or punish. Instead, they choose Oneness over separateness. They are committed to the team's success and achieving team goals.

To overcome a battleground in yourself or your team, go to RightMindedTeamwork.com, or visit your favorite book retailer to pick up your copy of *How to Apply the Right Choice Model: Create a Right-Minded Team That Works as One*. Inside, you will find a list of battleground attitudes and behaviors as well as the costs and benefits of classroom versus battleground thinking and behaving.

Certified Master Facilitator (CMF)

The Certified Master Facilitator (CMF) credential is a mark of excellence for facilitators. It is the highest available certification for facilitators. To learn more or to find a certified facilitator worldwide, visit the International Institute for Facilitation at INIFAC.org.

Classroom:
Where People Learn from Mistakes

Like the battleground, the classroom is a symbol. But unlike the battlefield, where people punish or are punished, the classroom is where you learn and find inspiration.

At some point in your past, you have experienced the joy and wonder of learning. Right-Minded Teamwork invites you to view your team as a safe place to experience this wonder and joy as you learn new teamwork skills and collaborate to achieve team goals.

When you are experiencing fear in any form or realize you are having an Ego attack, you are in the battleground. To return to the classroom, say to yourself, *There is nothing to fear. In my mind, I choose to rise above this silly battleground and head to my Right-Minded classroom. There, we are committed to do no harm and work as one. There, we will find solutions.*

By recognizing the fear behind your Ego attack and reminding yourself to return to the classroom, you experience a **moment of Reason**. You also strengthen your Right-Minded thought system and restore yourself to Right-Minded Thinking.

In the RMT book *How to Apply the Right Choice Model: Create a Right-Minded Team That Works as One,* you will find a list of 30 Right-Minded and wrong-minded attitudes and behaviors, plus the associated costs and benefits to your team.

Communication Work Agreement

What you think – *your thought system* – drives your communication in one of two ways. You either communicate as a collaborative ally or as a competitive, dysfunctional, and emotionally immature adversary.

Teams that work as one and achieve their goals regularly seek out opportunities to improve communication. They take positive action by creating and living a Communication Work Agreement that describes their team's agreed-upon communication style.

Right-Minded communication is a core concept in the book ***Right-Minded Teamwork****: 9 Right Choices for Building a Team That Works as One,* available at RightMindedTeamwork.com or your favorite book retailer.

To create your team's Communication Work Agreement, follow the suggestions in the book ***How to Facilitate Teamwork Agreements****: A Practical, 10-Step Process for Building a Right-Minded Team That Works as One.*

In there, you will find two real examples of which one is a team Communication Work Agreement.

Create, Promote, Allow

These three concepts form the foundation of the *Right Choice Model's* essential question:

*How have I **created**, **promoted**, or **allowed** this situation to occur?*

Asking and honestly answering this question ensures teammates are "owning their part" in a difficult situation.

These three concepts are also integrated into *7 Mindful Training Lessons: Improve Teammate's Ability to Work as One with Right-Minded Thinking.*

High-performing Right-Minded Teammates always ask themselves this question because it leads them to solutions. It is a clear demonstration of the RMT motto, "**Do no harm. Work as one.**"

Critical Few: Complete Important Tasks First

When a team is stuck in the "full-plate syndrome," identifying and completing the critical few - those tasks that have the largest and most direct impact on the team's success - is key to moving forward.

At the root of the full-plate syndrome is the **team's collective fear**, driven by Ego, which declares you will get in trouble if you do not do it all… even though the truth is you can never do it all.

People who listen to Ego believe they do not have a choice. Rather than realistically prioritizing their workload, they punish themselves for failing to meet the unreasonable goal of completing everything. They drain their energy, lose their focus, and make mistakes. They become powerless, cynical, and burned out.

But Reason reminds us that we always have this choice:

We can either win by doing the critical few tasks, or we can lose by attempting to do everything.

Spend more time doing the right things right and let go of low-value tasks. Holding on to lower-value tasks is **not security**. It is **incarceration**.

The "critical few" concept is discussed in the book ***Right-Minded Teamwork***: *9 Right Choices for Building a Team That Works as One*.

See **Recognition: Make It Easy to Keep Going** for a related concept.

Decision-Maker: The Real You

Ken Wapnick, Ph.D., created the term "Decision-Maker" to define the "real you" in *A Course in Miracles*. For more on his work, visit FACIM.org.

Within Right-Minded Teamwork, the *Right Choice Model* uses the term "Decision-Maker" to describe the part of you that chooses to listen to and follow either the wrong-minded ways of Ego or the Right-Minded ways of Reason.

Your Decision-Maker is 100% responsible for who you choose to follow, what you choose to think, and how you choose to behave.

Right-Mindedness is achieved when you listen to and follow Reason. Listening means calming your Ego mind, trusting your intuition, and allowing space for a **moment of Reason** to arise.

When Right-Mindedness becomes an integral part of a team, the team consistently works together as one, doing no harm, within the forgiving Unified Circle of Right-Minded Thinking. When teammates do that, they are demonstrating and extending Right-Minded Teamwork to everyone.

To learn more about Reason, Ego, and the Decision-Maker, pick up the book ***Reason, Ego, & the Right-Minded Teamwork Myth****: The Philosophy & Process for Creating a Right-Minded Team That Works Together as One.*

Decision-Maker: Trust Your Intuition

If thinking about Reason and Ego is new to you, it can be helpful to think of Reason as your positive intuition and Ego as your negative, arrogant, and sometimes vindictive intuition.

At different times throughout our lives, we all have listened to and followed each of these teachers.

Stop and remember when you had a hunch or a feeling as to what you should do or say in a particular situation. Did you ignore your intuition? Let's say you did not follow your instinct, and it turned out to be a mistake. What did you say to yourself and others?

I wish I had trusted my intuition!

As this memory illustrates, **you already know how to listen and be mindful** of your intuition. It is your natural, pre-separation state of mind [See **Oneness vs. Separateness**].

You just need to do it regularly.

Decision-Making Work Agreement

Every team needs a Decision-Making Work Agreement that clearly defines how decisions are made and who makes them. Creating a general agreement and putting it into your team's Operating System's Business Plan as a team Work Agreement makes good business sense.

If you do not currently have a Decision-Making team agreement or you have not updated it recently, I highly recommend you do that as soon as it is practical.

Incidentally, Decision-Making is #18 in the *Team Performance Factor Assessment* that you will use every 90 days to keep your team focused and on track. See **Team Operating System**.

In the book, ***How to Facilitate Team Work Agreements***: *A Practical, 10-Step Process for Building a Right-Minded Team That Works as One,* you will find two real agreement examples. The first one is a behavioral team Communication Work Agreement, and the other is a Decision-Making Work Agreement. Check it out and use it as a model for your team's Decision-Making Work Agreement.

Desire & Willingness: Preconditions for Accountability

Even though the terms "desire" and "willingness" are not often mentioned in Right-Minded Teamwork materials (except within the *Right Choice Model*), Right-Mindedness and accountability are virtually synonymous.

The concepts of desire and willingness permeate all RMT methods and processes simply because it is impossible to think in a Right-Minded way, behave with Right-Minded Accountability, and achieve Right-Minded Teamwork without a heartfelt desire and genuine willingness to do so.

The Right Choice Model found in the book ***How to Apply the Right Choice Model**: Create a Right-Minded Team That Works as One* teaches, *Right-Minded accountability is the desire and willingness to change my mind and behavior in order to effectively respond to difficult team situations.*

If you share the Right Choice Model with your team and distribute the Right Choice cards to teammates, you will see the definition of "desire and willingness" on the cards.

Do No Harm. Work as One.

The Right-Minded philosophy is founded on two universal truths:

Do No Harm.
Work As One.

None of us is as smart as all of us.
Right-Minded Teammates know that working collaboratively together, in a Right-Minded manner, is the only way to create the kind of teamwork that achieves and sustains 100% customer satisfaction. Said differently, these teammates genuinely want and need their fellow teammates.

Do no harm and work as one.
As a Right-Minded Teammate, you can be firm, direct, gentle, and compassionate, all at the same time. You do not blame yourself or others for mistakes. You and your teammates are allies, not adversaries, working together towards your shared goals.

Ego & Ego Attack

Ego is the negative, wrong-minded teacher who continually tells you how difficult the world is and how you must constantly fight to survive.

Reason is the opposite of Ego. Reason teaches you to *do unto others as you would have them do unto you.*

Ego believes everyone is out to get you and directs you to *do unto others before they do unto you.* Ego is also the creator of the tiny, mad idea of separation presented in the *Right-Minded Teamwork Myth*.

An Ego attack is a flash of negative, out-of-control emotion. It happens when you believe the awful feeling you are experiencing has been caused by something someone else said or did to you. Without thinking, you become behaviorally triggered; your body language, tone of voice, and the words you say become mean-spirited. An Ego attack is the opposite of a **moment of Reason**.

As soon as you realize you are experiencing an Ego attack, you must train your mind to say, *I am angry. I have lost control. I'm not upset for the reason I think. I am out of my right mind. I need a moment of Reason to gain control of my attitude. I must return to the classroom so I can find a Right-Minded way of replying that allows us to do no harm and work as one.*

Interlocking Accountability

Interlocking accountability is a crucial RMT concept that is primarily used in *How to Facilitate Team Work Agreements: a Practical, 10-Step Process for Building a Right-Minded Team That Works as One.*

When your team creates Work Agreements, it is highly recommended that one of your agreements includes an interlocking accountability statement so that teammates agree, ahead of time, how to compassionately confront a teammate who continues to break your Work Agreements.

Interlocking accountability means many things, including:

- Giving positive reinforcement when someone continues to do a great job of living the Work Agreements.
- Confronting someone in a supportive and safe but firm way if they continue to break the spirit or letter of the team's Work Agreement.
- Being accountable to each other for achieving or accomplishing the desired outcome of the Work Agreements.
- Recovering and learning from mistakes rather than denying or punishing those who make mistakes. This strengthens team spirit and trust.
- Creating and sustaining teammate trust because teammates who believe everyone will live their part of the Work Agreement will create Right-Minded Teamwork.

Moment of Reason

When you are facing a challenge such as an Ego attack, and you experience a positive and perhaps surprising moment of revelation, clarity, or sanity, you have achieved a moment of Reason.

These moments occur when you genuinely try to move from the battleground into the classroom. When Reason's teaching breaks through, you move from wrong-mindedness into Right-Mindedness.

Moments of Reason are magnificent. They are a cornerstone of your Right-Minded thought system. When they happen, you feel confident and at peace. You know what you should do, what to say, and to whom.

In moments of Reason, you know beyond a shadow of a doubt that you want and need your teammates. You easily return to the Unified Circle of Right-Minded Thinking, where teammates forgive one another, do no harm, and work as one.

Onboarding New Teammates

When a new leader or teammate joins your team, it is vitally important to properly onboard them within their first week on the job. In a single short meeting where everyone attends, the onboarding is easily and effectively accomplished.

Present all your RMT goals and Work Agreements along with why they were created. They ask you clarifying questions. Afterward, you ask them to accept the team's goals and actively live the team's Work Agreements.

Oneness vs. Separateness

Oneness is a psychological state of mind. It can be described in many ways using phrases such as *None of us is as smart as all of us,* or *do no harm,* and *work as one.*

Separateness is the opposite of Oneness. To become a Right-Minded teammate, you must train your mind to choose attitudes and behaviors that create and extend Oneness, not project separateness.

For a list of 30 examples of Oneness, see the Right-Minded Teamwork Attitudes & Behaviors list found in numerous RMT books.

The concepts and story behind Oneness and separateness are introduced in RMT's book, **Reason, Ego & the Right-Minded Teamwork Myth:** *The Philosophy and Process for Creating a Right-Minded Team That Works Together as One.*

In this book, you will learn about Ego's "tiny, mad idea" of wanting more "stuff" and how Ego's choices led us all into a world of separation. That tiny, mad moment was, literally, the **birth of separation**. But, as the Myth reveals, Reason is always ready to lead us back into Oneness - our pre-separation state – joyfully described as the Unified Circle of Right-Minded Thinking where we can do no harm and work as one.

Preventions & Interventions

In RMT's ***Design a Right-Minded, Team-Building Workshop****: 12 Steps to Create a Team That Works as One*, the team-building facilitator and team leader meet early on to proactively identify potential issues that could keep teammates from achieving the workshop's desired outcomes.

This discussion leads to creating *preventions* that the team leader or facilitator takes to help prevent those issues from happening. The facilitator and team leader also agree on how to intervene in case the preventions don't work. Much of the time, however, preventions do their job and make *interventions* during team-building workshops unnecessary.

To learn more about effective preventions and interventions, go to RightMindedTeamwork.com or your favorite book retailer, and pick up your copy of these two books:

How to Facilitate Team Work Agreements: *A Practical, 10-Step Process for Building a Right-Minded Team That Works as One*

Design a Right-Minded, Team-Building Workshop: *12 Steps to Create a Team That Works as One*

Psychological Goals

A team's psychological goals describe how teammates intentionally choose to think and behave as they work together to achieve their team's business goals.

Psychological goals, such as achieving mutual trust and respect among teammates, may be viewed as a team's collective school of thought, values, or thought system.

These consciously chosen goals, captured in team Work Agreements, clarify the team's principles or standards of behavior.

Here is a specific example of a psychological goal you will find in several RMT materials:

> *When difficult team situations happen, we accept, forgive, and adjust our attitudes and behavior. We always find solutions because we believe that none of us is as smart as all of us.*

Reason

Reason is a mythological character and symbolic guide who shows you how to think and behave in a Right-Minded way. As your Right-Minded teacher, Reason helps you differentiate and choose between Right-Minded and wrong-minded attitudes and behaviors.

Reason is the opposite of Ego. Whereas Ego believes everyone is out to get you and instructs you to *do unto others before they do unto you,* Reason teaches you to *do unto others as you would have them do unto you.*

Ego encourages and projects separateness.
Reason cultivates and extends Oneness.

Reason is that part of your mind that always speaks for the Right Choice attitudes and behaviors. When you need a **moment of Reason** to find the best way to respond to a difficult team situation, say to yourself:

> *I am here to be truly helpful.*
>
> *I am here to represent Reason who sent me.*
>
> *I do not have to worry about what to say or what to do because Reason who sent me will direct me.*

When you experience a moment of Reason (a moment of revelation, clarity, or sanity regarding a particular challenge), "remembering" Reason's gentle guidance towards Oneness restores your mind to the forgiving Unified Circle of Right-Minded Thinking.

For the full story of Ego's tiny, mad idea of separation and how Reason waits even today to bring us back to Oneness, pick up your copy of the book ***Reason, Ego & the Right-Minded Teamwork Myth****: The Philosophy and Process for Creating a Right-Minded Team That Works Together as One.*

Reason, Ego & the Right-Minded Teamwork Myth

This book teaches two significant concepts:

- the Right-Minded Teamwork Myth is a short tale that presents RMT's underlying teamwork philosophy of doing no harm and working as one
- the Right-Minded Teamwork team-building tools, methods, and processes to create Right-Minded, productive teams.

The RMT Myth is a short, simple story. It follows three characters: Reason, Ego, and you, the Decision-Maker. Simply put, the RMT Myth and philosophy advocate for teammates to follow Reason's path of Oneness instead of following Ego's disastrous advice to seek separateness and prioritize selfishness.

Following the RMT Myth, you will learn about the Right-Minded Teamwork process. Unlike the story, the RMT process is no myth. It is practical, deliberate, and reliable.

The RMT process is a set of interconnected, team-building methods that together form a self-perpetuating, continuous improvement system. This process allows you to integrate the aspirations of the RMT Myth into your team in a way that helps you achieve your business goals.

This book teaches the RMT process and provides a clear overview of the seven other RMT team-building books that, when used together, form a continuous improvement process guaranteed to support team growth and success.

Recognition:
Make It Easy to Keep Going

Authentic recognition is not about bestowing company shirts and prizes. It is about giving and receiving genuine appreciation for a job well done.

Recognition plays a critical role in growing your team's business because it keeps your team's spirit ignited. Unfortunately, many people work in team environments where there is little to no recognition. These teammates are discouraged. They do not give their best to the team. Why should they?

Discouraged teammates are like racehorses. If a horse is giving you only 80%, you can whip him, and he will give you 90%. Whip him again, and he will give you 100%. But if you whip him again, after he has already given you everything he has, he will drop back to 80%, or maybe even less. He has learned that you are going to whip him regardless, even if he works harder. So why should he give you his best?

Whipped people leave teams.

Far too often, the ones who leave are the most talented teammates. People who receive legitimate and genuine recognition stay and contribute. Shirts and prizes cannot earn that kind of loyalty or effort.

In the book ***Right-Minded Teamwork****: 9 Right Choices for Building a Team That Works as One*, you will learn that Recognition is one of the 9 Right Choices.

See **Critical Few: Complete Important Tasks First** for a related concept.

Right Choice Model

The *Right Choice Model* is an effective teaching aid that will help you and your teammates choose your own set of unique, "right" teamwork attitudes and behaviors.

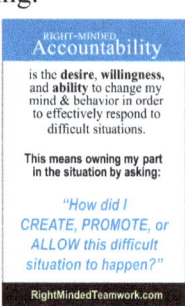

Inspired by *A Course in Miracles*, *The Right Choice Model* consists of two circles. The upper loop of acceptance, forgiveness, and adjustment represents the Unified Circle of Right-Minded Thinking.

The lower loop of rejection, Ego attack, and defensiveness describes the separated or divided circle of wrong-minded thinking.

To learn more about this simple but powerful teaching model, go to RightMindedTeamwork.com or your favorite book retailer, and pick up your copy of ***How to Apply the Right Choice Model****: Create a Right-Minded Team That Works as One*.

Right-Minded Teamwork's 5-Element Framework

Right-Minded Teamwork is a business-oriented, psychological approach to team building where acceptance, forgiveness, and adjustment are teammate characteristics, and 100% customer satisfaction is the team's result.

Right-Minded Teamwork is built off a framework of 5 Elements consisting of two goals and three teamwork methods.

1. Team **Business Goal**: Achieve 100% Customer Satisfaction
2. Team **Psychological Goal**: Commit to Right-Minded Thinking
3. Team **Work Agreements**: Create & Follow Commitments
4. **Team Operating System**: Make It Effective & Efficient
5. **Right-Minded Teammates**: Strengthen Individual Performance

To learn more, go to RightMindedTeamwork.com or your favorite book retailer, and pick up your copy of ***Right-Minded Teamwork in Any Team***: *The Ultimate Team-Building Method to Create a Team That Works as One.*

Right-Minded Teamwork's 5 Element Implementation Plan

There is no one right way to implement RMT's 5 Elements but the three-workshop plan presented in the book ***Right-Minded Teamwork in Any Team***: *The Ultimate Team-Building Method to Create a Team That Works as One* has proven effective countless times.

Here's a brief overview.

First Workshop
Create **psychological goals** plus at least one **Work Agreement**.

Second Workshop
Reaffirm **business goals** and agree on a **team operating system**.

Third Workshop
Encourage and support Right-Minded **Teammate development**.

After the third workshop, and every 90 days after that, you will apply RMT's ***Team Operating System & Performance Factor Assessment*** to identify opportunities, take action, and achieve new teamwork improvements.

Right-Minded Teamwork Attitudes & Behaviors

The Right-Minded Teamwork model includes a list of 30 behavioral and process-oriented teammate attitudes and behaviors with their associated costs and benefits. I collected and compiled these over three decades of team-building workshops.

This valuable list includes clear, specific, right, and wrong behaviors "taught" to us by either Reason or Ego.

Thoughts and attitudes always precede teamwork behavior. Right-Minded attitudes come from Reason. Wrong-minded attitudes come from Ego.

The good news is that Right-Minded attitudes are natural. They are already inside you and your teammates. When you think about any of the wrong-minded Ego attitudes listed you will see in the list, ask yourself,

> *Was I born with these depressing, debilitating, and awful attitudes?*

Your answer will always be **"no!"** You learned those wrong-minded attitudes from Ego. That means *you can unlearn them, too*.

You can find the list in several RMT books, including ***How to Apply the Right Choice Model****: Create a Right-Minded Team That Works as One*, available at RightMindedTeamwork.com or your favorite book retailer.

Right-Mindedness vs. Wrong-Mindedness

"Mindedness" is what you choose to think and perceive. Right-Mindedness refers to the positive mental state, perceptions, choices, and actions you demonstrate when following Reason's guidance.

Wrong-mindedness refers to the negative mental state that occurs when you follow Ego's advice.

> *Mindfulness is a journey without distance to a goal **you want to achieve.***

In the book ***How to Apply the Right Choice Model***: *Create a Right-Minded Team That Works as One*, you will find a list of rewards and consequences for choosing Right-Mindedness.

In the book ***7 Mindfulness Training Lessons***: *Improve Teammates' Ability to Work as One with Right-Minded Thinking*, you will learn that in every circumstance, and especially during difficult team situations, Right-Minded Teammates practice mindfulness, or Right-Mindedness, to move them into an ally-focused way of thinking and behaving.

Both of these books will help you accept that your mind is split between two thought systems. At one moment, you are following Reason, and the next, Ego. It is impossible to create and sustain Right-Minded Thinking with a split mind. To heal your split mind, you want to apply the *7 Mindful Training Lessons* and the *Right Choice Model's* attitudes and behaviors.

To bring your team back into the forgiving Unified Circle of Right-Minded Thinking, pick up your copy of these books at your favorite book retailer or RightMindedTeamwork.com.

RMT Facilitator

The RMT Facilitator has a special function. Simply put, their expert facilitation *transforms* well-meaning dysfunctional souls into *healthy and functional teammates*.

Using the array of RMT tools, the RMT Facilitator guides teammates in converting their team mistakes into *do-no-harm-work-as-one* attitudes and behaviors.

Teammates are perpetually grateful for the RMT facilitator's help in achieving and sustaining Right-Minded Teamwork. Some even say their RMT Facilitator *saved them*. Team leaders and teammates continually seek the RMT Facilitator's support for years to come.

Team transformations are the RMT Facilitator's **special function**.

Team Management System: An RMT Enterprise-Wide Process

An enterprise's Team Management System (TMS) aligns all teammates' attitudes and work behavior throughout the organization. An effective TMS ensures everyone is doing their part to help the organization achieve the enterprise's vision, mission, and strategic goals.

RMT's Team Management System involves integrating RMT's 5-Element Framework into all teams.

1. Team **Business Goal**: Achieve 100% Customer Satisfaction
2. Team **Psychological Goal**: Commit to Right-Minded Thinking
3. Team **Work Agreements**: Create & Follow Commitments
4. **Team Operating System**: Make It Effective & Efficient
5. **Right-Minded Teammates**: Strengthen Individual Performance

To learn more, go to RightMindedTeamwork.com or your favorite book retailer, and purchase your copy of *Achieve Your Organization's Strategic Plan: Create a Right-Minded, Team Management System to Ensure All Teams Work as One.*

Team Operating System & Performance Factor Assessment

RMT's Team Operating System is a six-step, 90-day, continuous improvement operating system that organizes your team functions to increase the likelihood of achieving customer satisfaction.

The system also includes the *Team Performance Factor Assessment* [step 3], which you will use to help teammates identify two to three improvement opportunities every 90 days.

The 25 performance factors in this assessment are aligned with and thus measure the six steps of RMT's Team Operating System. They effectively measure all aspects of Right-Minded Teamwork.

If you want your team to operate more effectively and efficiently, apply this 90-day process after your team has completed the first three RMT workshops. For a brief explanation, see the glossary: *Right-Minded Teamwork's 5-Element Implementation Plan*.

Apply the three-workshop plan and the operating system, and you nearly guarantee your team will create Right-Minded Teamwork.

To learn the process, go to RightMindedTeamwork.com or your favorite book retailer, and pick up your copy of **Right-Minded Teamwork in Any Team:** *The Ultimate Team-Building Method to Create a Team That Works as One.*

Thought System

What you believe *is* your thought system. Pause and reflect on this truth, and above all, be thankful that it is true.

Whether you are consciously aware of it or not, your thought system is the lens through which you view the world. Without exception, everyone has one. And though there are many variations, there are ***only two thought systems*** from which to choose:

- A Right-Minded thought system, which extends ally beliefs of acceptance, forgiveness, and adjustment to everyone, everywhere, forever
- A wrong-minded system, which projects adversarial assaults of rejection, attack, and defensiveness to everyone, everywhere, forever

Once you have developed a thought system of any kind, you live it and teach it. Even if you are not entirely aware of it, it remains at the forefront of your mind, influencing your daily behaviors and choices.

If your thought system is negative, or you choose to follow Ego into an unnecessary and adversarial competition, you cannot be a happy, successful teammate.

To live in the land of Oneness where your workplace is a safe and supportive classroom and where you and your teammates work as one to achieve team goals, you must train your mind and align your thought system with the teachings of Reason.

There is no possible compromise between these two thought systems. You either collaborate, or you compete. When you follow Ego, you take your team to the battleground. When you choose to follow Reason, you willingly create and genuinely strive to live your team's Work Agreements. With Reason's help, you transform your team into a lovely, collaborative, successful classroom.

The choice is clear.

Reject Ego. Embrace Reason.

Be Thankful.

Train Your Mind

When your mind is well-trained in Reason's Decision-Making ways, Ego attacks do not throw you off course. When a difficult team situation happens, you immediately stop for a **moment of Reason**. You refocus on Oneness, rise above the battleground, and remember to live your Work Agreements in your classroom.

To train your mind simply means practicing your team's Work Agreements, which represent your psychological goals, as often as possible, especially during difficult team situations.

Uncovering Root Cause

The Right-Minded Teamwork philosophy advocates leaders, teammates, and facilitators resolve the root cause of teamwork issues instead of making the mistake of addressing symptoms.

Though this view is discussed in many RMT materials, uncovering the root cause is heavily emphasized as a core concept in the book ***Design a Right-Minded, Team-Building Workshop***: *12 Steps to Create a Team That Works as One*.

Inside that book, you will find a story about a well-meaning team leader who asked me, as their team-building facilitator, if I could teach a three-day workshop in just two days. He believed a quick team event would address the problem he saw in his team.

But the problem he was seeing was only the symptom, not the root cause of the issue. Had I agreed and given him what he asked for, the team would still be struggling with the same issue. And, as a facilitator, I would have failed both the team and the leader.

Instead, by pausing to look for the root cause of the team challenge first, we ended up designing and executing a practical, Right-Minded Teamwork workshop to solve the actual underlying problem.

By seeking out the root cause first, we delivered the leader's desired result, even though the workshop we held was not what he had initially asked for.

To improve your ability to uncover root causes and read this short story, go to your favorite book retailer or RightMindedTeamwork.com and pick up your copy of ***Design a Right-Minded, Team-Building Workshop***: *12 Steps to Create a Team That Works as One*.

Unified Circle of Right-Minded Thinking

When your team discusses and agrees on your psychological goals – your consciously chosen set of attitudes and behaviors as described in your Work Agreements – you have created your team's collective thought system.

By uniting with each other in this way and openly committing to one another through your Work Agreements, you are renouncing Ego in yourself and your teammates and collectively committing to train your minds to follow Reason.

This process of creating team Work Agreements is your undivided declaration of interdependence. Your assertion is saying,

> *We hold these mindful truths to be self-evident that all minds are created equal, and whosoever believes that will have everlasting freedom to choose Right-Minded Teamwork.*

Your declaration plus your daily acts of living your team Work Agreements ***is your return*** to the forgiving Unified Circle of Right-Minded Thinking.

Work Agreements

A Work Agreement is a collective promise made by teammates to transform non-productive, adversarial behavior into collaborative teamwork behavior. Work Agreements are a key tool for teammates and teams who aspire to do no harm and work as one.

Work Agreements are not flimsy ground rules. They are emotionally mature work performance commitments. Work Agreements announce your dedication to Oneness and demonstrate your inner belief that *none of us is as smart as all of us.*

Your team's collective Work Agreements also define your team's psychological goals and thought system. They ensure you conduct your day-to-day work from within your team's Unified Circle of Right-Minded Thinking.

To learn more about the power of Work Agreements and how to use them to transform your team, go to RightMindedTeamwork.com or your favorite book retailer, and pick up your copy of **How to Facilitate Team Work Agreements**: *A Practical, 10-Step Process for Building a Right-Minded Team That Works as One.*

Resources

To download RMT models and processes to give teammates, go to RightMindedTeamwork.com, and search for this book's companion ***Reusable Resources & Templates***.

> **Reusable Resources & Templates**
>
> *for*
>
> **How to Apply the Right Choice Model**
>
> Create a Right-Minded Team That Works as One
>
> DAN HOGAN

The End

Thanks for reading our Right-Minded Teamwork book. If you enjoyed it, wouldn't you please take a moment to leave a review at your favorite retailer or RightMindedTeamwork.com?

And finally, on behalf of Reason and all the Right-Minded Teammate Decision-Makers, we extend our best wishes to you and your teammates as you create another Right-Minded Team that works together as one.

HOW TO APPLY THE RIGHT CHOICE MODEL · 193

www.ingramcontent.com/pod-product-compliance
Lightning Source LLC
Chambersburg PA
CBHW072010110526
44592CB00012B/1253